Editors:
Professor John Curtice, Miranda P

BRITISH SOCIAL ATTITUDES 33

NatCen
Social Research that works for society

British Social Attitudes 33

NatCen Social Research

At NatCen Social Research we believe that social research has the power to make life better. By really understanding the complexity of people's lives and what they think about the issues that affect them, we give the public a powerful and influential role in shaping decisions and services that can make a difference to everyone. And as an independent, not for profit organisation we're able to focus our time and energy on meeting our clients' needs and delivering social research that works for society.

Publication details
Curtice, J., Phillips, M. and Clery E. (2015), British Social Attitudes: the 33rd Report, London: NatCen Social Research, available online at: www.bsa.natcen.ac.uk

First published 2016

NatCen Social Research
35 Northampton Square
London
EC1V 0AX
info@natcen.ac.uk

Contents

Foreword

In this, NatCen's 33rd annual British Social Attitudes report, we endeavour to uncover the consequences of seven years of austerity for social and political attitudes in Britain.

The financial crash of 2008 and the "great recession" that followed left a lasting impression on the British economy that included slower economic growth, declining living standards and stagnant wages.

The political response has been a period of austerity in the form of public spending cuts and tax increases. Changes to the benefits system and the way we are taxed have, according to the Institute for Fiscal Studies (IFS), reduced household incomes by £1,127 a year.1 The IFS also says this austerity is set to continue, even deepen further, under the current administration until the end of the decade at least. Now that the UK has voted to leave the European Union, even further spending reduction and tax increases may be in train.

We know then that the British public has been hit in the pocket, but what impact has this had on the way we view the world, our attitudes and perceptions of society, and our expectations of government? There are a variety of ways that the public could have reacted, and, of course, different people may react differently. But in financially straightened times, have we become more sympathetic to those who have less or do our personal financial worries take precedence? Has austerity divided the rich from the poor, the working class from the middle class? Have stagnant wages made us unhappy at work, or more grateful to have a job? Have we become more demanding of politicians or have we withdrawn from the political process?

NatCen's latest British Social Attitudes survey seeks to answer these questions - and more - by looking at the effect of austerity on attitudes in five important areas: class, benefits, work, the NHS and politics.

Responding to austerity

The recent period of austerity does seem to have affected the views of at least some British people – though not always in a straightforward fashion.

We find Britain divided along class lines. Nearly 8 in 10 of us think that the divide between social classes is wide or very wide. We are less likely now to think it possible to move between social classes than in the past, reflecting, perhaps, the fact that social mobility is not what it once was.

We observe a reaction against cuts in the form of increased support for higher spending on benefits for people who are disabled and single parents. But towards people without a job, especially those who don't have children, the public remains unsympathetic.

Perhaps counter-intuitively for a period of comparatively slow wage growth, more people are positive about the quality of their jobs than

1 (REF: http://www.ifs.org.uk/uploads/publications/bns/BN159.pdf)

in the past. And more people too tell us that they would work even if they did not need the money.

But there are also indicators that not everyone is finding work better than before – and certainly not easier. In particular, people in routine and semi-routine occupations are more likely to feel stress and less likely to have flexibility in the workplace than ten years ago – at a time when people in other occupations are more likely to feel they have control over their working day.

Divided on the policy response

Austerity has then seemingly made a difference, but when we examine how the public would like government to respond to the country's financial predicament, we find them more divided than in the past.

The EU Referendum has highlighted some sharp divisions in British society and the closeness of the result presents a very definite challenge about how government can keep large minorities happy. We see similar challenges when it comes to what people want government to do on public spending.

After having apparently failed to make an impact for some time, austerity does now seem to have awakened support for higher public spending; more people want an increase in spending than for a decade. Here we draw on one of the longest running and most revealing questions on the survey. For ten years a majority have said that public spending should not be increased, yet now the public is evenly split over whether there should be more spending or whether it should remain at the same level.

Attitudes to taxation and spending on health, education and social benefits, 1983–2015

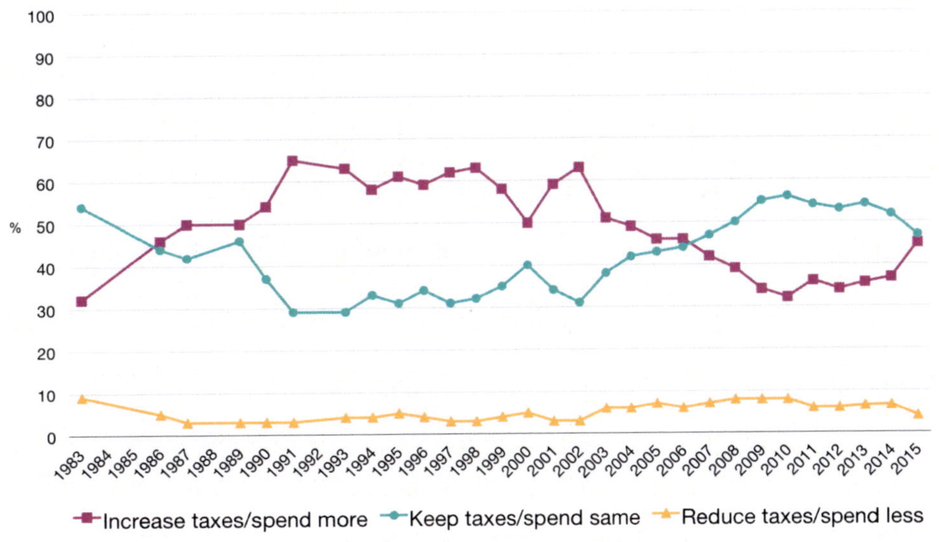

This division over public spending also extends to what it should be spent on. We all (93% of us at least) recognise that the NHS is facing a funding crisis – and increasing taxes is the single most popular solution. However, many people prefer other solutions, including the NHS simply learning to live within its means. Meanwhile, even on a policy such as the spare room subsidy, where if you believed the popular narrative you might think it was universally despised, a large minority, and in particular young people, are in favour.

The more things change…

We see then that austerity has had an impact on public attitudes, and not just the pound in our pockets. But, at the same time, some things have not changed at all. The public's sense of social class has withstood dramatic long-term changes in the labour market. As many as 60% of us describe ourselves as working class, (including half of people in managerial and professional occupations) almost exactly the same proportion as in 1983.

We have been through a period of intense public debate about Britain's constitution in the form of the Scottish Independence referendum, English votes for English laws, and a dramatic General Election (the survey was carried out a little under a year before the EU Referendum). So are people more interested in constitutional change? Not necessarily. While support for electoral reform, for example, appears to have reached an all-time high, it is still only a minority preference.

Meanwhile, although austerity appears to have had a discernible impact on attitudes, for the most part the changes are not big attitudinal leaps, but rather small steps. This is of course usually how attitudes change. But a cohesive democracy should worry about a public that describes society as divided by class and says social mobility is decreasing, especially if the jobs of those at the bottom are getting worse while those of others get better or if the public is gradually losing faith in the electoral system. We must think about how we can find consensus on a way forward for the health service and the welfare state. Because with austerity expected to continue until at least 2020 these small steps might well add up to a leap.

Kirby Swales

Director, NatCen's Survey Research Centre

Social Class

Identity, awareness and political attitudes: why are we still working class?

Despite a long-term decline in the size of the working class, the proportion of the public who identify themselves as working class has remained stable over time. This chapter explores the reasons for this apparent contradiction and its implications for social and political attitudes and politics more generally.

Majority consider themselves working class

Despite a decline in the number of routine and semi-routine workers in Britain, a majority of people still identify as working class.

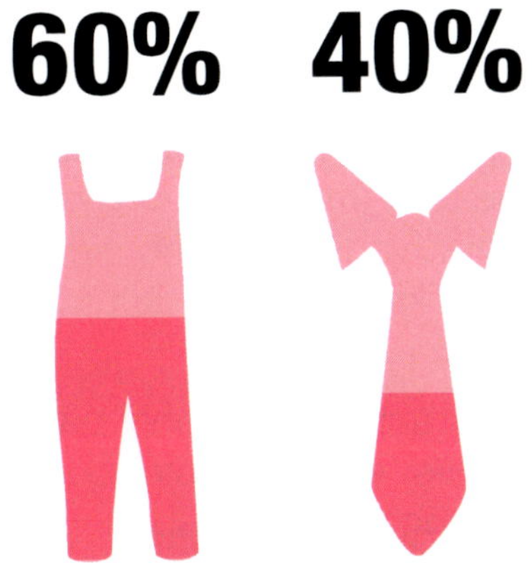

60% say they are working class, compared with 40% who say they are middle class. This proportion who consider themselves working class has not changed since 1983.

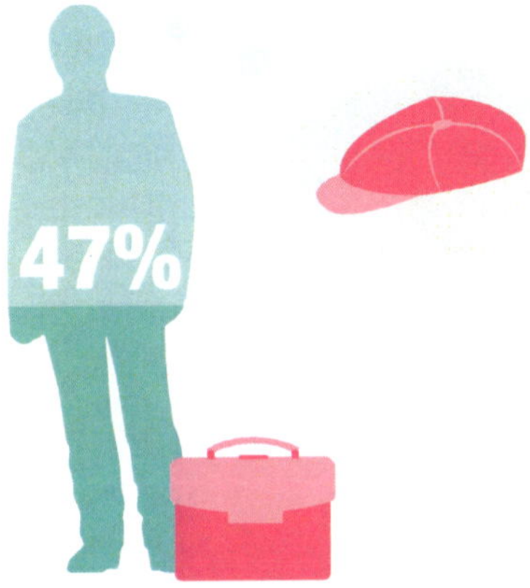

Just under half (47%) of those in jobs classified as managerial and professional consider themselves working class.

Class identity links with wider attitudes

Those who identify as working class tend to express distinct attitudes on immigration and social issues.

Those who identify as working class are more likely than those who identify as middle class to say that there is a wide divide between social classes (82% compared with 70%).

People who see society as divided between a large disadvantaged group and a small privileged elite feel more working class regardless of their actual class position.

Occupationally middle class people who feel they are working class do not differ in their attitudes towards redistribution from other middle class people but are much more like the working class on immigration and social issues.

Author

Geoffrey Evans, Nuffield College, University of Oxford
Jonathan Mellon, Nuffield College, University of Oxford

Introduction

Almost 20 years ago, just before Labour won the 1997 election, John Prescott supposedly announced that 'we're all middle class now' and Tony Blair stated that his "historic mission" was "to liberate Britain from the old class divisions, old structures, old prejudices".[1] In the boom time of the 2000s with rising house values, a surging economy and a surplus of public money to be spent on the provision of social services, people just might have believed this was or could be true. But in post-crisis, post-recession Britain, with stagnant wages, part-time working, and zero-hours contracts, these ideas seem rather less plausible.

Nevertheless, many reputable sources have catalogued the decline of the working class in modern Britain. According to the Office for National Statistics (ONS) and numerous academic analyses, the working class has been shrinking to a fraction of its former size. Official statistics make clear that what they call 'routine and semi-routine workers' no longer form the largest group in society. This change is, perhaps, not surprising given the dramatic decline of Britain as a manufacturing powerhouse and the rise of China and others as the suppliers of goods. In the advanced economies of the modern globalised world, manual workers in manufacturing industries are an endangered species.

There is a big difference between being working class as defined by officials and social scientists in terms of occupation and being working class as defined by people themselves

But the number of manual workers in Britain today is only part of the picture. There is another working class: what we might call the working class of the mind. Though working class occupations are usually thought to amount nowadays to only around a quarter of the population (as discussed in our chapter on Work), 60% still claim to be 'working class' when asked to express a class identity (Heath et al., 2013). There is a big difference between being working class as defined by officials and social scientists in terms of occupation and being working class as defined by people themselves.

In this chapter we examine why this difference exists and its implications. Why do so many people in the professional and managerial occupations see themselves as working class? What are the implications of this for their social and political attitudes, and for politics more generally? The modern Labour Party moved away from its old working class rhetoric and appeals. Under Tony Blair it decided that the name of the game was appealing to the middle classes. But if the self-defined middle class is a minority is this the right thing to do? Can the politics of anti-austerity, such as that promulgated by the current Labour leader, Jeremy Corbyn, prove a successful strategy for appealing to the self-defined working class? Conversely, can the politics of anti-immigration do likewise for a leader such as Nigel Farage? Or does whether people identify as working class make less difference to their political attitudes and choices than whether or not they actually are in manual occupations?

1 Blair stated this in his Labour conference leader's speech in 1999. Prescott denies having made this oft-quoted claim however: http://www.theguardian.com/theguardian/2012/aug/05/corrections-and-clarifications.

Is social class about what people do or what people say?

Our focus on these questions is a response to a great deal of commentary and research that argues that in modern societies, (i) class identity has become of little importance and (ii) class position no longer influences how people see themselves and others (Beck and Beck-Gernsheim, 2002). According to this perspective, traditional notions of social class simply do not resonate with ordinary people's experience of social life. A strand of this argument claims that working class people, in particular, have lost their sense of class identity, and that their sense of self no longer represents a distinctive expression of their social position and no longer informs their beliefs about politics and society (e.g. Savage et al., 2010). Other researchers, in contrast, have claimed that rather than class identity disappearing, most people simply follow John Prescott: they believe they are middle class.[2] As we shall see, neither perspective appears to be accurate.

Class identity and awareness

By class identification we simply mean the tendency for people to place themselves in a social class. It is distinct from 'class awareness', which is present when people believe that class position has important consequences, that there are barriers between classes, and that social class still has an impact on their own and others' lives (Vanneman and Cannon, 1987). We begin by assessing whether the prevalence of class identification has changed in recent years before turning to how class aware people appear to be.

The British Social Attitudes (BSA) survey has asked people whether they identify with a particular class on a number of occasions in recent years. There are two stages to the question, and we ask respondents:

> ***Do you ever think of yourself as belonging to any particular class?***
>
> ***If yes: Which one is that?***
>
> ***If no (or yes, but other than middle or working class): Most people say they belong to either the middle class or to the working class. Do you ever think of yourself as being in one of these classes?***

In the top half of Table 1 we show the proportion who say they are middle or working class in response to the initial question, together with the proportion who say they do not identify with a particular class. In the bottom half we show the proportion who say they are

2 The idea that everyone is becoming middle class has been a common theme in response to the growth of affluence in modern societies and also draws on the idea that social comparison processes with people around us result in self-placement in the middle of social hierarchies (Kelley and Evans, 1995). However, there is speculation that the recent economic crisis has re-shaped class perceptions because the pressures associated with recession heighten class awareness (Oddsson, 2010) and strengthen the impact of occupational class on class identity (Haddon, 2014), while at the same time increasing inequalities are serving to polarise class identities (Andersen and Curtis, 2012).

middle or working class in response to either the initial or the follow-up question, leaving aside the small proportion (3% in 2015) who still say they are neither middle nor working class.

Table 1 Class identification, 2003–2015

	2003	2005	2006	2012	2015
Unprompted	%	%	%	%	%
Middle	19	20	20	22	20
Working	27	26	33	29	23
None	54	54	48	48	57
Unweighted base	*947*	*2063*	*3230*	*1044*	*1079*
Prompted	%	%	%	%	%
Middle	38	39	38	37	40
Working	62	61	62	63	60
Unweighted base	*932*	*1966*	*3105*	*1028*	*1053*

Table 1 shows that, when responding to our initial question, people are slightly more likely to say they are working class than middle class. However, when those who did not identify a class at our initial question are prompted to choose between these two options, overall people are significantly more likely to identify as working class than middle class (6 in 10 compared with 4 in 10). Moreover, the proportion saying they are working class has barely changed at all during the last dozen years. Furthermore, when we compare these results with answers to the same question collected as part of the British Election Study (BES) in 1983, 1987, 1992 and 1997, we find that the proportion identifying themselves as working class has barely changed in the past 33 years; in 1983 this proportion was 60%, while 34% identified themselves as middle class (although these proportions should be marginally lower, as those not identifying with a social class, even when prompted, were included in the base) (Heath et al., 2013).

The proportion identifying themselves as working class has barely changed in the past 33 years

Even though the proportion of people doing a working class job has declined, the level of identification with the working class has proven to be a remarkably stable feature of British society. Moreover, this experience stands in stark contrast with that of the United States, where the proportion of people identifying as working class has tracked the decline in the proportion engaged in working class occupations, with the consequence that more people now regard themselves as middle class than working class (Hout, 2008).[3]

But does this continuing sense of working class identity also mean that people are 'class aware'? That is, is a working class identity associated with a belief that there are important differences and

3 Hout's (2008) long-term analysis of the American National Election Studies (ANES) found there was a predictable shift in line with changes in class sizes: In the 1950s 40% of respondents placed themselves in the middle class and 60% in the working class. By 2000, 59% said "middle class" and 41% working class. There is hardly any such pattern observable for Britain over the same period (Heath et al, 2009; Evans and Tilley, 2017).

boundaries between classes? We can begin to address this issue, by examining how people responded when they were asked:

> ***How difficult would you say it is for people to move from one class to another?***
>
> ***Very difficult,***
>
> ***Fairly difficult,***
>
> ***Not very difficult***

Only a minority think that it is "not very difficult" to move between classes, and at just over a quarter, the proportion that do take that view has dropped from a little over a third in 2005

As shown in Table 2, in truth, only a minority think that it is "not very difficult" to move between classes, and at just over a quarter, the proportion that do take that view has dropped from a little over a third in 2005. This decline is consistent with the claim that the change in the economic climate between 2005 and 2015 has served to make people more aware of class differences. Meanwhile, it is also the case that those who identify as working class are rather more likely to believe movement between classes is "very difficult". People's class identity is, on this measure at least, linked to some extent with their class awareness.

Table 2 Perceived difficulty of moving between classes, by class identity, 2005 and 2015

Class identity (prompted)		Very difficult	Fairly difficult	Not very difficult	*Unweighted base*
2005					
Middle class	%	13	47	40	*700*
Working class	%	23	46	32	*1121*
All	%	19	46	35	*1857*
2015					
Middle class	%	17	54	30	*443*
Working class	%	25	51	24	*615*
All	%	21	52	26	*1058*

This last point is affirmed if we examine the responses to two questions on how wide the divide between the classes is that were asked in our most recent survey:

> ***How wide are the differences between social classes in this country, do you think?***
>
> ***Very wide,***
>
> ***Fairly wide,***
>
> ***Not very wide,***
>
> ***No differences between classes***

and:

> ***Do you think these differences have become greater or less or have remained about the same?***
>
> ***Greater differences,***
>
> ***About the same,***
>
> ***Less differences***

As the first part of Table 3 shows, almost no one believes there are no differences between classes, while 21% think either that there are no differences or that the differences are not very wide. Working class identifiers (18%) are less likely than those who identify as middle class to think there are either no differences or that they are not very wide (30%). Meanwhile, as shown in the second part of Table 3, rather more people (31%) think that social differences have become greater than believe they have become less (24%). Middle class identifiers (32%) are notably more likely than their working class counterparts (19%) to feel that differences have become less.

Table 3a Perceived differences between social classes, by class identity

Class identity (prompted)		Very wide	Fairly wide	Not very wide	No difference between classes	*Unweighted base*
Middle class	%	20	50	27	3	*445*
Working class	%	27	55	16	2	*634*
All	%	24	53	21	2	*1079*

Table 3b Perceived trend in differences between social classes, by class identity

Class identity (prompted)		Greater difference	About the same	Less difference	*Unweighted base*
Middle class	%	26	42	32	*445*
Working class	%	35	46	19	*634*
All	%	31	44	24	*1079*

A majority of people appear to perceive that there are class divisions and boundaries in British society

So class identity, and especially working class identity, is alive and well. At the same time, a majority of people appear to perceive that there are class divisions and boundaries in British society. Moreover, those who identify as working class are more likely to be aware of these divisions and boundaries. But what influences how people place themselves in classes?

What are the sources of working class identity?

We first examine how far class identity varies according to the jobs that people do and thus the occupational class to which sociologists and statisticians think they belong. For this purpose we define three occupational classes using the established (NS-SEC) class schema that has been developed by the ONS (see Technical Details for more information). These are employers, managers, professionals and higher supervisors (who may be regarded as the middle class), intermediate, small employers, own account workers, lower supervisory and lower technical workers (intermediate class) and routine and semi-routine workers (working class). Table 4 shows the proportion of those in each of these three occupational classes who identify as working class. That proportion has remained relatively stable over the last decade: consistently around 4 in 5 objectively working class people identify as working class, as do just under half of objectively middle class people. The proportion of intermediate workers who identify as working class tends to fall somewhere in between these two groups. In short, almost half of those who are objectively middle class identify as working class and this has shown no sign of changing in recent years.

Table 4 Working class identity by occupational class, 2003–2015

% identifying as working class	2003	2005	2006	2012	2015
Occupational class					
Managerial and professional	44	43	44	43	47
Intermediate, self-employed and lower supervisory	70	68	70	73	64
Semi-routine and routine	77	76	78	81	77
Unweighted base	*907*	*1908*	*3014*	*990*	*1050*

So why is there such a gap between the prevalence of class identity, the occupational classifications of the ONS, and John Prescott? One possibility is that although occupationally middle class people say they are working class they do not mean it as strongly. They might call themselves middle class but they do not really believe they have a lot in common with working class people. This possibility can be assessed by examining people's answers to the following question:

> ***Some people feel they have a lot in common with other people of their own class, but others don't feel this way so much. How about you? Would you say you feel ... pretty close to other [middle/working] class people, or, that you don't feel much closer to them than you do to people in other classes?***[4]

4 Those who said they were middle class were asked how close they were to middle class people, while those who identified as working class were asked about their closeness to working class people.

Table 5 Reported closeness to those who share the same class identity, by occupational class, 2005 and 2015

		Class identity				
		Working class		Middle class		
Occupational class		Feel close to other working class people	Do not feel close to other working class people	Feel close to other middle class people	Do not feel close to other middle class people	*Unweighted base*
2005						
All	%	24	37	23	16	*1843*
Managerial & professional	%	13	29	33	25	*657*
Intermediate, self-employed and lower supervisory	%	26	42	19	13	*649*
Semi-routine & routine	%	35	41	17	8	*537*
2015						
All	%	28	30	25	17	*1006*
Managerial & professional	%	17	27	33	24	*402*
Intermediate, self-employed and lower supervisory	%	32	31	23	14	*315*
Semi-routine & routine	%	40	34	16	10	*289*

Among those in a semi-routine or routine (working class) occupation, on balance rather more (40%) say that they feel close to other working class people than say they do not (34%)

Table 5 reveals there is some apparent truth to our supposition. Among those in a semi-routine or routine (working class) occupation, on balance rather more (40%) say that they feel close to other working class people than say they do not (34%). In contrast, among those in professional and managerial (middle class) occupations, the balance is in the other direction (17% say they feel close but 27% that they do not). This replicates a not dissimilar pattern that was previously in evidence in 2005. It appears that those who are occupationally working class who also identify as working class are more likely to feel closer to the working class than do occupationally middle class people who claim to be working class.

Many of those in middle class jobs who claim to be working class, do in fact come disproportionately from working class backgrounds

One possible reason why this might be the case is that those in middle class occupations base their judgments on how close they feel to other working class people on different criteria to those employed by people in working class occupations. In particular, someone who themselves is in a middle class occupation but whose parents were in working class jobs may still claim to be working class, but perhaps feel that they do not have as much in common with those who have not been occupationally upwardly mobile. Certainly, as Table 6 shows, many of those in middle class jobs who claim to be working class, do in fact come disproportionately from working class backgrounds. No less than 61% of those in a professional or managerial job, and whose father was in a routine or semi-routine job, describe themselves as working class, compared with just 24% of those whose father occupied a similar position to themselves. A similar pattern is evident among those who are occupationally intermediate class, although relatively small base sizes for these categories mean that these findings should be treated with caution.

Table 6 Proportion identifying as working class, by father's occupational class and respondent's occupational class

% identify as working class		Father's occupational class	
Respondent's occupational class	**Father: managerial and professional**	**Father: intermediate, self-employed and lower supervisory**	**Father: semi-routine and routine**
Managerial and professional	24	49	61
Intermediate, self-employed and lower supervisory	36	69	73
Semi-routine and routine	‡	68	75

‡ = percentage not shown as base is less than 50

The bases for Table 6 can be found in the appendix to this chapter

So family background matters to people's class identity and given that 14% of the managerial and professional class are from working class backgrounds (and an additional 29% are from what we term intermediate class backgrounds) this goes a long way to explaining the continuing sense of being working class among many people in middle class jobs. Other factors matter too though. Educational attainment is intimately bound up with occupational achievement and people's understanding of class position (Robinson and Kelley, 1979; Stubager et al., 2016). It would be surprising if educational attainment didn't shape someone's sense of class identification even within occupational classes. Table 7 shows how education makes a difference within occupational classes: the impact of having a degree is strong within the managerial and professional and intermediate occupational classes, but insufficient respondents in the working class (6%) have degrees for reliable estimates to be calculated.

Table 7 Proportion identifying as working class, by educational level and respondent's occupational class, 2012 and 2015 combined

% identify as working class	Respondent's highest educational qualification			
Respondent's occupational class	**None**	**O level**	**A level**	**Degree**
Managerial and professional	‡	50	49	28
Intermediate, self-employed and lower supervisory	70	68	69	40
Semi-routine and routine	75	75	76	‡

‡ = percentage not shown as base is under 50

The bases for Table 7 can be found in the appendix to this chapter

People who see themselves as at the bottom of a structure in which there are a few super rich and then everyone else might well think of themselves as 'working class' relatively speaking even if they do hold a middle class job

Images of inequality

That social background and educational qualifications matter for an individual's class self-concept regardless of their current job makes sense from what we know about psychological research about how self-concepts are formed. However, this may not be the only reason why those in middle class occupations are divided in their sense of class identity. The failure of many people in middle class occupations to regard themselves as middle class can also be, in part, understood by looking at how people visualise the structure of our society.

People who see themselves as at the bottom of a structure in which there are a few super rich and then everyone else might well think of themselves as 'working class' relatively speaking even if they do hold a middle class job. The emphasis in the popular media on the lives of the super-rich, on the earnings and bonuses of bankers, and on the surprisingly large sums of money paid to managerial staff even in the public sector, might well result in these phenomena becoming a yard stick or even a grievance. We can examine this possibility by looking at the answers to a question asked as part of the 2009 survey.[5] Respondents were shown five diagrams of different types of society, together with brief summaries of what they represented. These are shown in Figure 1.

Figure 1 Images of Society[6]

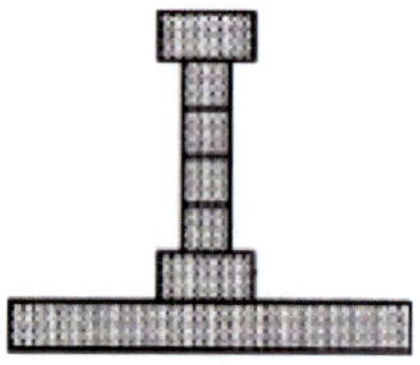

Type A
A small elite at the top, very few people in the middle and the great mass of people at the bottom.

Type B
A society like a pyramid with a small elite at the top, more people in the middle, and most at the bottom.

Type C
A pyramid except that just a few people are at the bottom.

Type D
A society with most people in the middle.

The most popular view of society was Type B (a society like a pyramid with a small elite at the top, more people in the middle and

5 This question is part of a module on inequality fielded as part of the International Social Survey Programme (ISSP) and has been asked in some countries since the late 1980s (Evans et al., 1992) as a way of gauging people's view of their society's structure of inequality.

6 Another image of society that was also included – 'an upside down pyramid' - is not shown because it was not seen as plausible: only 30 respondents picked it.

most at the bottom); this was chosen by 41%. Twenty per cent of people in each case selected Type C and Type D, while 15% chose Type A.

Those middle class people who see society as a division between a large disadvantaged group and a small privileged elite are much more likely to regard themselves as working class (59%) than are those who see society as either having relatively few people at the bottom (16%) or even most people in the middle (16%)

Table 8 show the proportions among those who selected each of the images of society who identify as working class. Our analysis indicates that people who see society as a division between a large disadvantaged group and a small privileged elite are much more likely to regard themselves as working class (66%) than are those who see society as either having relatively few people at the bottom (28%) or even most people in the middle (26%). These patterns are echoed even more strongly within the middle class itself. Middle class people who see society as a division between a large disadvantaged group and a small privileged elite are almost as likely to see themselves as working class (59%) as are people in general, whereas only very few (16%) of those who see society as having relatively few people at the bottom or most people in the middle do so. However, caution must to be applied to these findings due to the small sub-samples involved. If this analysis is correct, it is quite possible that occupationally middle class people who think of themselves as working class believe they are part of a large and relatively disadvantaged group. The salience in the media of the super-rich, city bankers, and chief executives of big companies can plausibly make even the middle classes feel that they are in fact still part of the working class.

Table 8 Proportion identifying as working class, by respondent's occupational class and perceived image of society, 2009

Image of society	Managerial, professional and intermediate	All
	% identify as working class	
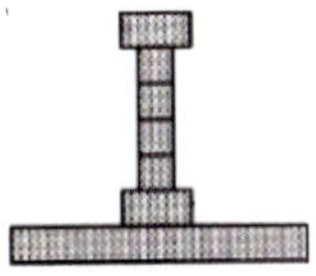	59	66
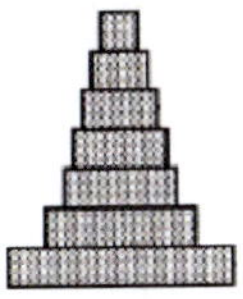	31	46
	16	28
	16	26

The bases for Table 8 can be found in the appendix to this chapter

Class identity and political attitudes

But does any of this matter when it comes to people's social and political attitudes? Are these attitudes influenced at all by the class with which people identify? One way of addressing this question would be to examine the link between class identity and party choice. However, this would not necessarily be that informative as parties, especially the Labour Party, have in recent decades radically changed their class image.[7] Instead, therefore, we examine the link between identity on the one hand and values and attitudes on the other. People's values and attitudes are less constrained by the nature of the policies that parties represent. They tell us about what people would like to see happen regardless of what the main political parties offer. Among the subjects in the 2015 survey where attitudes might be thought to be influenced by class identity, are the questions that comprise our regular 'left-right' scale. This scale includes questions about inequality and redistribution, such as whether "Government should redistribute income from the better-off to those who are less well off", whether "Big business benefits owners at the expense of workers", and the survey's libertarian-authoritarianism scale that captures attitudes towards such issues as the death penalty, homosexuality and morality (see Technical Details for the full details of both these scales). We can also examine attitudes to a particularly important current issue - immigration.

In Table 9 we show how attitudes towards these three subjects vary both by occupational class and class identity. For ease of interpretation we dichotomise the various scales. A right-wing response is coded as an average score of greater than 2.5 on the five item left-right scale (where the values range from 1, meaning very left-wing, to 5, very right-wing), and authoritarian is coded as greater than 3.6 on the five item libertarian-authoritarianism scale (where again the values range from 1, very libertarian, to 5, very authoritarian) (Evans, Heath and Lalljee, 1996). Similarly, on immigration, respondents who choose between 6-10 in response to the question "On a scale of 0 to 10, where 0 is extremely bad and 10 is extremely good, would you say it is generally bad or good for Britain's economy that migrants come to Britain from other countries?" are coded as pro-immigrant, whereas those who choose a response between 0-5 are coded as anti-immigrant.

7 Evans and Tilley (2017) show how for much of the 20th century Labour was regarded as the party of the working class, and regarded itself as such, but by 1997 New Labour was explicitly rejecting such linkages. Class voting dropped accordingly (Evans and Tilley, 2012). Party choice is therefore no longer a good guide to measuring the implications of class identity.

Table 9 Libertarian-authoritarian and left-right values and attitudes towards immigration, by occupational class and class identity

		Liber-tarian	Author-itarian		Left	Right		Anti-immigrant	Pro-immigrant
Occupational class									
Managerial and professional	%	59	41	%	44	56	%	46	54
Intermediate, self-employed and lower supervisory	%	39	61	%	51	49	%	65	35
Semi-routine and routine	%	40	60	%	58	42	%	69	31
Class identity									
Middle class	%	55	45	%	40	60	%	48	52
Working class	%	40	60	%	49	51	%	65	35

The bases for Table 9 can be found in the appendix to this chapter

Those in routine and semi-routine occupations are more left-wing, authoritarian and anti-immigrant than those in professional and managerial jobs

Those in routine and semi-routine occupations are more left-wing, authoritarian and anti-immigrant than those in professional and managerial jobs. They disagree about immigration and on libertarian-authoritarian values in particular, while the division between them on left-right values is rather less sharp. Thus, for example, whereas a majority (69%) of those in routine and semi-routine occupations hold anti-immigrant views, a majority of those in professional and managerial occupations (54%) are pro-immigrant in their stance on the subject. Meanwhile, on both immigration and libertarian-authoritarian values those in intermediate occupations hold almost identical views to those in working class jobs. At the same time, the balance of opinion among those who identify as working class is also more likely than among those who consider themselves to be middle class to be left-wing, authoritarian and anti-immigrant, and again especially so in respect if the latter two.

However, on its own Table 9 does not tell us whether class identity makes any difference to people's attitudes. Perhaps the differences in attitudes by class identity simply arise out of the fact that those who identify as working class are disproportionately engaged in routine and semi-routine occupations. As such, it is important to take into account the overlap between occupational and subjective class and see if the latter still matters substantially. In Table 10 we show what happens when we take into account someone's occupational class and their class identity simultaneously. For each combination of occupational class and class identity it shows, first, the proportion who are right-wing; second, the proportion who are authoritarian; and third, the proportion who are pro-immigrant. Thus, for example, the 59% figure in the top left-hand corner of the table means that 59% of those in professional and managerial occupations who identify as middle class are classified as right-wing. Meanwhile as 60% of those in the same occupational group who identify as working class are right-wing, this means that class identity does not make any difference to the prevalence of right-wing values among those who are in professional and managerial occupations.

Table 10 Prevalence of right-wing, authoritarian and pro-immigrant attitudes, by occupational class and class identity

	Managerial and professional	Intermediate, self-employed and lower supervisory	Semi-routine and routine	*Unweighted base*
% right-wing				
Middle class identifier	59	61	59	*378*
Working class identifier	60	47	47	*524*
% authoritarian				
Middle class identifier	38	55	49	*381*
Working class identifier	56	60	63	*526*
% pro-immigration				
Middle class identifier	64	42	34	*427*
Working class identifier	38	32	31	*610*

This, however, is not the general message of the table. Rather it is the exception. Within each occupational class, those who identify as working class are more likely to be authoritarian and less likely to be pro-immigrant. At the same time, with the singular exception of those in professional and managerial occupations, those who identify as working class are also less likely to be right-wing in their values. All of these effects prove to be significant when modelled statistically.[8] Evidently while having a working class identity and being middle class does not make you more likely to want to redistribute wealth, it does make you more authoritarian and less pro-immigrant and thus in these subjects at least more likely to have an outlook that is very similar to that of those who are occupationally working class.

Conclusions

Working class identity remains widespread in Britain. Even though only a minority of people are engaged in working class occupations, a majority of us still think of ourselves as working class. Those in middle class occupations still think of themselves to a surprising degree as working class, and especially so if their family background was working class or they have never been to university. And this sense of working class identity apparently means that they are less libertarian and less pro-immigrant, but not necessarily more left-wing

8 These differences are generated using a logistic regression. The percentage differences are the marginal effect of being in each of the class groups versus being in the manager/professional class and being a working class identifier versus a middle class identifier. All of the differences are significant at the 5% level.

The current sources of working class identity amongst those in middle class jobs may now be beginning to dry up

– even though those with a working class identity are particularly likely to think that class differences and barriers remain important.

So contrary to the expectations of some academic researchers, social class still has resonance for people, we are clearly not 'all middle class now'. However, the current sources of working class identity amongst those in middle class jobs may now be beginning to dry up. The 'golden age' of upward social mobility in the second half of the 20th century saw many people from working class backgrounds end up in middle class jobs (Bukodi et al., 2015). However, that transformation of the occupational structure has now very much slowed, if not stalled completely. As a result, the proportion of first generation people in the middle classes who come from working class backgrounds is set to fall. Meanwhile, the proportion in middle class occupations who have higher educational qualifications is set to rise as the massive increase in higher education over the last few decades works its way through the cohorts that occupy middle class jobs – jobs that are far more dependent on educational qualifications for access than they used to be. Working your way up from the shop floor without educational qualifications is not the norm in today's credentialist society.

Between them these processes would lead one to expect working class identification to decline among those in middle class jobs. As a result, we should see a closer match between class identity and objective class. This would ensure that social attitudes become more libertarian, but not more economically right-wing - and are thus be likely to be more sympathetic to Labour and the Liberal Democrats. The decline of working class identity and the further decline of left-wing politics are unlikely to go hand in hand.

References

Andersen, R. and Curtis, J. (2012), 'The Polarizing Effect of Economic Inequality on Class Identification: Evidence from 44 Countries', *Research in Social Stratification and Mobility* **30(1)**: 129–41

Beck, U. and Beck-Gernsheim, E. (2002), *Individualization: Institutionalized Individualism and its Social and Political Consequences*, London: Sage

Bukodi, E., Goldthorpe, J.H., Waller, L. and Kuha, J. (2015), The mobility problem in Britain: new findings from the analysis of birth cohort data, *The British Journal of Sociology* **66(1)**: 93 – 117

Evans, G. and Tilley, J. (2012), The Depoliticization of Inequality and Redistribution: Explaining the Decline of Class Voting, *Journal of Politics,* **74(4)**: 963-976

Evans G. and Tilley J. 2017.*The New Politics of Class in Britain: How the Working Class have been Excluded from British Politics*. Oxford: Oxford University Press.

Evans, G., Heath, A.F. and Lalljee, M.J. (1996), 'Measuring left-right and libertarian-authoritarian values in the British electorate, *British Journal of Sociology*, **47**: 93-112

Evans, M.D.R., Kelley, J. and Kolosi, T. (1992), 'Images of Class: Public Perceptions in Hungary and Australia', *American Sociological Review,* **57(4)**: 461–82

Haddon, E. (2015), Class identification in New Zealand: An analysis of the relationship between class position and subjective social location, *Journal of Sociology*, **51(3)**: 737–754

Heath, A.F., Curtice, J. and Elgenius, G. (2009), Individualization and the decline of class identity, pp. 21-40 in Wetherell, M. (ed.) *Identity in the 21st Century: New Trends in Changing Times*, Basingstoke: Palgrave

Heath, A.F., Savage, M. and Senior, N. (2013), 'The role of class in shaping social attitudes', *British Social Attitudes: the 30th Report*, London: NatCen Social Research

Hout, M. (2008), 'How Class Works: Objective and Subjective Aspects of Class Since the 1970s', pp. 25–64 in A. Lareau and D. Conley (eds.), *Social Class: How Does it Work?,* New York: Russell Sage Foundation

Jackman, Mary R., and Jackman, David W. (1983), *Class Awareness in the United States,* Berkeley: University of California Press

Kelley, J. and Evans, M.D.R. (1995), "Class and Class Conflict in Six Western Nations", *American Sociological Review,* **60**: 157-178

Oddsson, G.A. (2010) 'Class Awareness in Iceland', *International Journal of Sociology and Social Policy,* **30(5/6)**: 292–312

Robinson, R.V. and Kelley, J. (1979), 'Class as Conceived by Marx and Dahrendorf: Effects on Income Inequality and Politics in the

United States and Great Britain', *American Sociological Review,* **44(1)**: 38–58

Savage, Mike, Silva, Elizabeth and Warde, Alan (2010), Cultural *analysis and Bourdieu's legacy*: settling accounts and developing alternatives, pp 60-74, in Silva, Elizabeth and Warde, Alan (eds.), Culture, Economy and the Social, London: Routledge

Stubager, R., Tilley, J., Evans, G. and Robinson, J. (2016), "In the eye of the beholder: What determines how people sort others into social classes?", Paper presented at the MPSA annual conference, Chicago April 7th-10th

Vanneman R., and Cannon, L.W. (1987), *The American Perception of Class,* Philadelphia, PA: Temple University Press

Acknowledgements

NatCen Social Research is grateful to The Danish Research Council (grant number 1327-00113), Jesus College Major Research Grants Fund and Nuffield College for their financial support which enabled us to ask the questions reported in this chapter. The views expressed are those of the authors alone.

Appendix

Bases for Table 6 are as follows:

Table A.1 Bases for Proportion identifying as working class, by father's occupational class and respondent's occupational class, 2015

% identify as working class	Father's occupational class		
Respondent's occupational class	**Managerial and professional**	**Intermediate, self-employed and lower supervisory**	**Semi-routine and routine**
Managerial and professional	*150*	*118*	*113*
Intermediate, self-employed and lower supervisory	*77*	*116*	*119*
Semi-routine and routine	*38*	*91*	*145*

Bases for Table 7 are as follows:

Table A.2 Bases for Working class identification by educational level and respondent's occupational class, 2012 and 2015.

% identify as working class	Respondent's highest educational qualification			
Respondent's occupational class	None	O level	A level	Degree
Managerial and professional	*41*	*122*	*255*	*346*
Intermediate, self-employed and lower supervisory	*155*	*190*	*202*	*78*
Semi-routine and routine	*263*	*179*	*106*	*19*

Bases for Table 8 are as follows:

Table A.3 Bases for Proportion identifying as working class, by respondent's occupational class and image of society

Image of society	Managerial, professional and intermediate	All
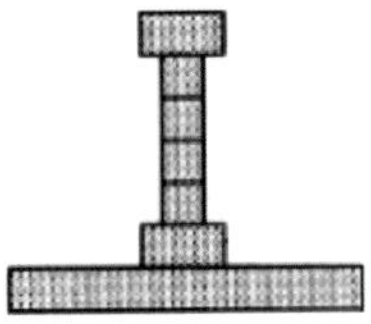	*50*	*131*
	*171*	*371*
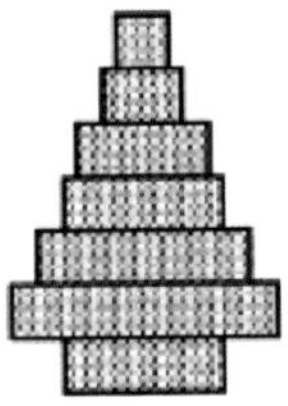	*102*	*170*
	*98*	*184*

Bases for Table 9 are as follows:

Table A.4 Bases for left-right and libertarian-authoritarian values and attitudes towards immigration by occupational class and class identity

	Libertarian/ authoritarian	Left/right	Anti-immigrant/pro-immigrant
Occupational class			
Managerial and professional	*1419*	*1419*	*810*
Intermediate, self-employed and lower supervisory	*1098*	*1089*	*639*
Semi-routine and routine	*988*	*986*	*610*
Class identity			
Middle class	*402*	*398*	*449*
Working class	*539*	*536*	*640*

Welfare

Support for government welfare reform

This chapter examines support for two key elements of government welfare reform and whether and how this has changed since its implementation began in 2010: reducing expenditure on welfare; and limiting the circumstances in which particular benefits can be received. It assesses how attitudes vary and whether these are primarily influenced by characteristics linked to 'ideology' or 'self-interest'.

Little support for reducing spending for most groups

There is minimal support for reducing welfare spending, except in relation to the unemployed and low income working couples without children.

45%
support less government spending on unemployed people

7%
support less government spending on retired people

31% disagree that "the government should spend more money on welfare benefits for the poor".

61% think a working-age couple without children who are struggling to make ends meet should look after themselves, rather than the government topping up their wages.

More support for limiting circumstances in which benefits can be received

A majority support limiting the circumstances in which unemployment benefit can be received, although there is less support for this approach in relation to housing benefit.

60% think that the duration of unemployment benefit should be limited.

40% think that the money a working-age couple receive from the government to help them pay their rent should be reduced if they have more bedrooms than the government thinks they need.

Attitudes vary by ideology and self-interest

Support for reform is strongly influenced by measures of ideology (such as political party identification). Measures of self-interest (such as age) also have a role to play. The importance of different characteristics varies in relation to different elements of reform and benefit types.

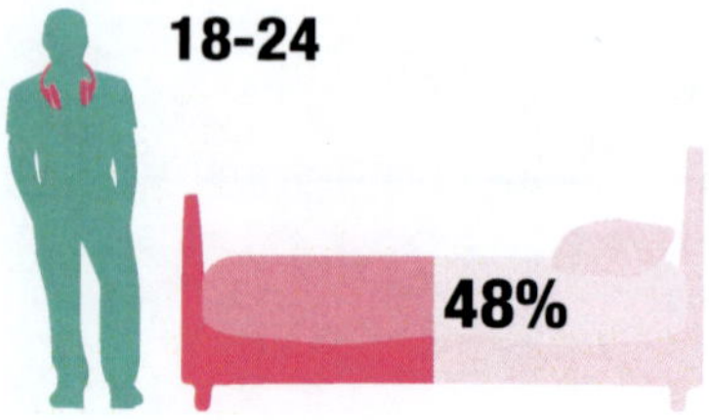

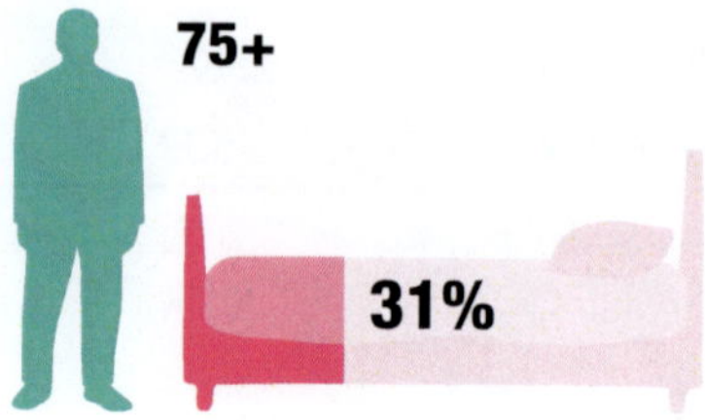

48% of those aged 18-24 think the money a couple receives to help them pay their rent should be reduced, if they have more bedrooms than the government thinks they need, compared with 31% of those aged 75+.

Author

Elizabeth Clery, Research Director, NatCen Social Research

Introduction

Since the General Election of 2010 the British government, first in the form of a Conservative-Liberal Democrat Coalition and latterly a majority Conservative government, has sought to implement a wide-ranging programme of welfare reform. One of the key aims of this programme has been to reduce expenditure on welfare, as part of the government's overall objective of cutting the public sector deficit. At the beginning of the Coalition's time in office the Chancellor, George Osborne, made a commitment to achieve cuts of 18 billion pounds to welfare expenditure by 2014-15 (HM Treasury, 2010 and 2013), a target that in practice was almost achieved.[1] Meanwhile, the Conservative Party's manifesto for the 2015 election committed the new majority Conservative government to making a further reduction of 12 billion pounds a year by 2017-18 (Conservative Party, 2015).

Introducing welfare reform has not been without its difficulties and controversies. There has been widespread criticism of a reduction that has been made to the housing benefit paid to social housing tenants who are deemed to be living in accommodation that contains more bedrooms than they need. Widespread retesting of the capabilities of those in receipt of disability benefits in order to assess whether they still need their current level of support has attracted particular criticism too. Meanwhile an attempt in the autumn of 2015 to limit eligibility for tax credits, a benefit paid to those in low paid jobs, was rejected by the House of Lords and subsequently dropped by the Chancellor. Most recently, proposed changes to Personal Independence Payments (PIP), a payment intended to cover the cost of meeting the care needs of people with disabilities, led to the resignation of the then Work and Pensions' Secretary Iain Duncan Smith, and the subsequent shelving of the proposed changes.

The extent of the controversy that has been engendered by the government's reform programme raises questions about the extent to which the public actually supports the objective of reducing welfare expenditure

The extent of the controversy that has been engendered by the government's reform programme raises questions about the extent to which the public actually supports the objective of reducing welfare expenditure. Have those politicians who have objected to various aspects of the government's reform package read public opinion accurately? After all, even if the public were initially in favour of reducing expenditure on welfare, perhaps the deeper the cuts have become, the more the public have reacted against them? Or are the government's critics misguided in their apparent belief that the public dislike the reductions in expenditure on welfare? Is there indeed, as the Conservatives appear to believe, an appetite for more?

Using data from the 2015 British Social Attitudes (BSA) survey, we address these questions by assessing the extent to which the public currently support two key strands of the government's

1 The reduction in spending on welfare achieved between 2010 and 2015 has been estimated at 16.7 billion for 2015-16 (Hood and Phillips, 2015).

programme of welfare reform, and examining how far attitudes are different now from what they were when the Conservative-led Coalition first came to power in 2010. Firstly, we assess attitudes towards the government's overarching aim of reducing the overall level of expenditure on welfare. Secondly, we assess how the public views one of the key approaches to achieving this aim, that is, limiting the circumstances in which particular benefits can be received. This may involve reducing the length of time for which a benefit is paid, limiting who is eligible to receive a benefit, or making tighter the conditions that have to be satisfied before a benefit is paid out.

In the first part of this chapter we consider the attitudes of the public as a whole towards welfare reform, examining a wide range of questions in order to obtain as complete a picture as possible of the nature and extent of support for reform. In the second part, we consider whether and how attitudes towards different elements of welfare reform varies across different demographic groups and how this variation might best be understood. In particular, we assess whether attitudes towards welfare reform are largely shaped by people's ideological outlook or by their self-interest. We conclude by considering the implications of our findings for the future of the government's reform programme.

Does the public support a reduction in welfare spending?

Our initial task, then, is to assess how much support there is for reducing the overall level of spending on welfare, and whether the level of support has changed since the Conservatives first came to power. We do so by examining, first, attitudes towards the overall level of spending on welfare and, second, attitudes towards specific benefits and potential recipients.

Overall spending on welfare benefits

As part of a suite of questions designed to measure public attitudes to the welfare state (see Technical Details for further information), each year we ask respondents how far they agree or disagree with the proposition that "The government should spend more money on welfare benefits for the poor". This statement is, of course, the opposite of the stance taken by the government, but how people respond to the proposition still gives us insight into attitudes towards the overall size of the welfare bill.

Figure 1 Attitudes to spending more on welfare benefits for the poor, 1987–2015

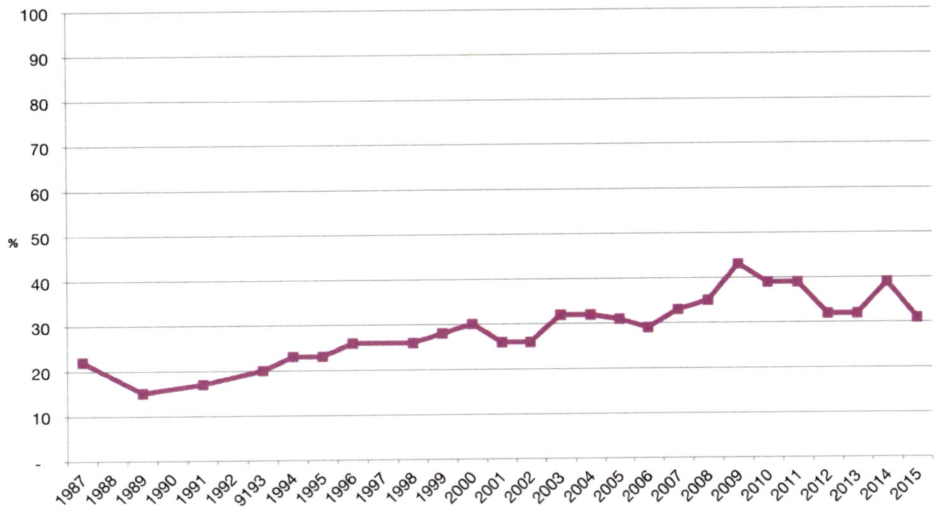

The data on which Figure 1 is based can be found in Table A.1 in the appendix to this chapter.

There is as yet insufficient evidence to conclude that the public have begun systematically to react against the cuts that have been implemented so far

Figure 1 shows that around one-third (31%) now disagree with this statement – and can thus be regarded as holding a view that is potentially consistent with the direction of welfare reform. However, this group could also include those who think that spending on this area should simply remain at current levels rather than be cut. Moreover, those belonging to this group are outnumbered by the 4 in 10 who agree that more money should be spent, while another 3 in 10 neither agree nor disagree. On this evidence it would appear that a majority of the public are unsympathetic to cuts to spending on welfare benefits. Moreover, the proportion who disagree that the government should spend more on welfare benefits for the poor is lower now that it was in 2010, although fluctuations up and down in that proportion since 2010 mean that there is as yet insufficient evidence to conclude that the public have begun systematically to react against the cuts that have been implemented so far. What, however, does seem to have ended is the gradual increase in the proportion opposed to more welfare spending that was in evidence before the Coalition came to power.

Spending on specific groups of benefit recipients

However, in truth, the government has not sought to curb all forms of welfare expenditure. Its focus has been on benefits paid to those of working age. Although the state pension age has been increased, otherwise benefits for pensioners have been protected; the government introduced a 'triple lock' for the state pension in 2011, guaranteeing that it would rise by whichever is the highest of the annual increase in earnings, prices, or 2.5%. Perhaps this selectivity reflects a public opinion that distinguishes between welfare for those still deemed to be of an age to work and those who are thought already to have done their bit for the economy? Or maybe people have come to feel that pensioners are being treated too favourably?

In Table 1 we show the proportion who say there should be "more spending" or "less spending" on six different groups of benefit recipients. As the second half of the table shows, in most cases there is little support for cutting benefits. Fewer than 1 in 10 support cutting benefits for carers, the disabled, those on low incomes – and, indeed, the retired. Well under 2 in 10 support less government spending on benefits for single parents. The one instance where there is considerable, though still less than majority, support for reducing benefits is in respect of the unemployed.

Table 1 Attitudes to government spending on different benefits, 1998–2015

	1998	2002	2004	2006	2008	2011	2013	2015
% would like to see more government spending on benefits for...	%	%	%	%	%	%	%	%
...people who care for those who are sick or disabled	82	82	81	82	83	74	73	75
...parents who work on very low incomes	68	69	62	66	67	58	59	61
...disabled people who cannot work	72	69	63	62	61	53	54	61
...retired people	71	73	73	72	72	57	48	49
...single parents	34	39	35	38	37	29	31	36
...unemployed people	22	21	15	16	14	15	15	17
	1998	**2002**	**2004**	**2006**	**2008**	**2011**	**2013**	**2015**
% would like to see less government spending on benefits for...	%	%	%	%	%	%	%	%
...people who care for those who are sick or disabled	1	1	1	1	1	1	1	2
...parents who work on very low incomes	3	4	4	4	4	5	5	5
...disabled people who cannot work	2	2	3	3	4	5	4	3
...retired people	2	2	2	2	2	3	7	7
...single parents	21	18	18	19	17	21	19	16
...unemployed people	35	36	44	45	54	51	49	45
Unweighted base	*3146*	*3435*	*3199*	*3240*	*3358*	*3311*	*3244*	*3266*

Moreover, there is some, albeit limited, evidence that views may have shifted somewhat in response to the cuts to spending on benefits undertaken to date. Support for reducing spending on benefits for unemployed people has fallen by six percentage points since 2011, and by nine points since 2008, despite the fact that unemployment has fallen in the interim. Meanwhile, after falling between 2008 and 2011, the level of support for increasing expenditure on those with a disability and on single parents has now returned to its pre-Coalition level. However, a similar drop between 2008 and 2011 in support for increasing spending on carers and those on low incomes has not been fully reversed, although the idea remains a relatively popular one.

The proportion who think that spending on retired people should be increased has fallen from 72% in 2008 and 59% in 2011 to slightly less than half (49%) now

Above all, however, the one group where the balance of opinion clearly has shifted is in respect of retired people. True, the proportion who would like to see less spending on this group has only increased from a very low 2% in 2008 to a still low 7% in 2015, but the proportion who think that spending should be increased has fallen from 72% in 2008 and 59% in 2011 to slightly less than half (49%) now. This fall is consistent with evidence presented in the 32nd report that retirement pensions are now less likely to be regarded as a priority for extra spending.[2] So while it appears that there is still little demand for reducing spending on the retired, it would appear that the public recognise that pensioners have been treated relatively well and that consequently they may no longer feel that there is a clear case for further increased spending on this group. That said, given that around a half still back increased spending on the retired, it can hardly be said that the government's policy on this subject flies in the face of public opinion.

So, it is only in the case of unemployed people that there is support for spending cuts, and even in this case that support is now somewhat lower than it was when the Coalition first came to power. In contrast, spending more on those who are in work but are on relatively low incomes apparently remains a relatively popular proposition. We evidently should look at attitudes towards the government topping up the wages of those on low incomes a little more closely.

Topping up wages

Since the introduction of tax credits in 1997, BSA has regularly ascertained people's views on this subject. We ask first:

> ***Some working couples with children find it hard to make ends meet on low wages. In these circumstances, do you think...***
>
> ***...the government should top up their wages,***
>
> ***...or, it is up to the couple to look after themselves and their children as best they can?***

Comparable questions are then asked about "working couples without children" and about "working lone parents".

Although 'making work pay' is a principle which underpins both the payment of tax credits and the government's welfare reform agenda, recent government reforms have, nevertheless, sought to reduce spending on tax credits. From April 2013, the rates of most

2 When respondents to the 2014 survey were asked for their first and second priorities for extra spending on social benefits, retirement pensions remained the most popular choice, although the proportion selecting this option as their first or second choice for extra spending had fallen from 78% in 2007 to 67% in 2014 (Taylor-Gooby, 2015).

working-age benefits, including tax credits, have risen by one per cent annually, rather than in line with inflation. More recently, the Chancellor has proposed lowering the earnings level at which tax credits begin to be withdrawn from £6,420 to £3,850, together with a speeding up of the rate at which withdrawal takes place – although, as noted earlier, these reforms were abandoned following their rejection by the House of Lords in 2015. Meanwhile the government has endeavoured to reduce the need to pay tax credits by trying to increase wage rates for the low paid; for instance, the Coalition's Programme for Government in 2010 included a commitment to introducing arrangement to protect those on low incomes from the effect of public sector pay constraints (Coalition, 2010). More recently it has increased the Minimum Wage, now entitled the National Living Wage, by more than that the rate of inflation, and proposes further such increases between now and 2020. Against this backdrop it seems reasonable to regard opposition to the idea of the government topping-up wages as evidence of support for the current direction of welfare reform.

Two-thirds back topping up the wages of lone parents, while well over half do so in respect of working age couples with children

Table 2 reveals that, in fact, attitudes depend considerably on the circumstances of the recipient. Two-thirds back topping up the wages of lone parents, while well over half do so in respect of working age couples with children. On the other hand, only a quarter believe the government should be topping up the wages of a couple without children. This pattern has been consistent ever since we first addressed the subject in 1998. It would seem that for many people the justification for paying benefit to the low-paid rests on whether or not it helps to reduce the harm that living in a low wage environment might do to the next generation, rather than because there is a perception that the government should be trying to limit the hardship suffered by the adults in question. But this of course implies that a blanket approach to cutting tax credits, as opposed to focusing on the support received by those without children, is at odds with public opinion.

Table 2 Support for topping up wages for different types of families, 1998-2015

	1998	2000	2003	2005	2010	2013	2015
Working couples with children	%	%	%	%	%	%	%
Government should top up their wages	56	61	59	58	55	59	55
Up to couple to look after themselves	31	28	29	31	31	29	29
Working couples without children	%	%	%	%	%	%	%
Government should top up their wages	25	27	26	26	27	28	25
Up to couple to look after themselves	58	63	63	64	62	59	61
Lone parent	%	%	%	%	%	%	%
Government should top up their wages	n/a	71	66	67	66	66	66
Up to parent to look after themselves	n/a	19	22	22	22	22	21
Unweighted base	*2531*	*2980*	*2649*	*1783*	*2791*	*2832*	*2781*

n/a = not asked

Only around 3 in 10 actually oppose increasing welfare spending on the poor

So far we have uncovered relatively little apparent support for the government's programme of welfare reform. Only around 3 in 10 actually oppose increasing welfare spending on the poor, that is the very opposite of what the government has been trying to achieve. There continues to be majority support for increasing spending on most groups of welfare recipients, and in some cases a drop in support for that view has subsequently been reversed. The one instance where there clearly has been a substantial reduction in support for more spending is in respect of the one group, retired people, who have largely been protected from the government's attempts to reduce expenditure. Only in the case of the unemployed and those on low wages who do not have children can it be claimed that the direction of public policy has been in line with that of public opinion. It would appear that apart from those two exceptions further cuts could well be met with considerable public controversy. However, what remains to be seen is whether or not this is the case for the second strand of welfare reform – that of limiting the circumstances in which benefits can be received.

Limiting the circumstances in which benefits can be received

We explore this by focusing on two particular benefits where the government has sought to restrict eligibility for benefit. The first is unemployment benefit,[3] for which a revised set of more stringent sanctions was introduced in 2012, with those who do not comply with them potentially losing all or some of their benefit for a period of time. The second is housing benefit, where the removal of the spare room subsidy in April 2013 means that those who are of working age and are deemed by the government to have more bedrooms than they need now have the amount that they receive to help them pay their rent reduced accordingly.

Reducing duration and eligibility for unemployment benefit

To measure support for the idea of limiting the duration of unemployment benefit, we first of all asked whether "a person who is receiving unemployment benefits" and "who is fit and able to work" should "receive unemployment benefits for as long as it takes them to find a job" or whether instead they "should only be able to receive unemployment benefits for a limited amount of time". The latter option is tighter than anything that has yet been proposed by the government, but nevertheless, as the first half of Table 3 shows, it is still the case that as many as three in five support the idea in principle, even if we cannot be sure what they think the limit should be. Moreover, there is no sign here of support having diminished over

3 While Jobseeker's Allowance was introduced in 1996 as the main welfare support for the unemployed (replacing unemployment benefits and income support), we use the term 'Unemployment Benefit' to describe generically the range of benefits for the unemployed that have existed across the lifetime of the survey.

time – if anything the opposite is true. On this topic it would seem there is considerable and consistent support for a relatively tough regime.

Just 3 in 10 think that the person with limited job skills should be required to look for work straight away, a figure that also has remained very stable over time

However, the picture looks a little different when we look at the responses to a second question in which respondents were asked whether "a person who is receiving unemployment benefits and who has limited job skills or work experience" should "be required to look for work straight away in order to continue receiving unemployment benefits" or instead "should be offered help to improve their job skills while continuing to receive benefits before they are required to look for work". Here just 3 in 10 think that the person with limited job skills should be required to look for work straight away, a figure that also has remained very stable over time. Perhaps the person who is trying to improve their job skills is thought to be making an effort that the person who is unemployed for a relatively long period of time is not.

Table 3 Attitudes to the duration of unemployment benefit receipt, 2007-2015

	2007	2009	2012	2015
Duration	%	%	%	%
Should receive for as long as it takes to find job	n/a	41	36	39
Should receive for a limited time	n/a	56	52	60
Person with limited job skills / work experience	%	%	%	%
Should be required to look for work straight away	31	30	33	31
Should be offered help to improve job skills while continuing to receive benefits	67	69	66	68
Unweighted base	*3082*	*3421*	*3248*	*3257*

n/a = not asked

But while the public may be sympathetic to the idea of someone being on benefit while enhancing their skills, they evince little support for the idea that an unemployed person should try to find the right job for them rather than the first job that comes along. This becomes clear when we asked respondents what should happen in various scenarios where a person on unemployment benefit was offered a job that was potentially unsuitable for them in some way. We asked respondents to:

> ***Imagine a person who is looking for work and receiving unemployment benefits. A job becomes available, which pays at least as much as they get in unemployment benefits, but it is not the kind of job they are looking for. For each of the following situations, please tell me whether you think they should take the available job, or remain on benefits while they look for a different job ...***
>
> ***...if the available job is paid at the minimum wage?***

...if the job is on a short-term contract?

...if it is a job they are not interested in?

As shown in Table 4, in each case, clear majorities of more than 8 in 10 think the person should take the job, rather than remaining on benefits to look for a different job. Moreover, that level of support has remained relatively stable. Although these questions do not tell us anything about what sanctions the public think should be imposed on someone who fails to take a job, they nevertheless suggest considerable support for the current direction of welfare reform – at least in relation to the unemployed.

Table 4 Views on whether person on unemployment benefits should take jobs that are unsuitable in some way, 2007-2015

	2007	2012	2015
Minimum wage job	%	%	%
Should take job	n/a	85	88
Should remain on benefits while they look for a different job	n/a	11	9
Short term contract	%	%	%
Should take	86	82	82
Should remain on benefits while they look for a different job	11	14	15
Job they are not interested in	%	%	%
Should take	79	83	83
Should remain on benefits while they look for a different job	16	14	14
Unweighted base	*3082*	*3248*	*3257*

n/a = not asked

However, we have already ascertained that attitudes towards benefits for the unemployed are not necessarily typical of attitudes towards welfare in general. We thus now turn to attitudes towards limiting access to housing benefit, and in particular to the principle behind the removal of the spare room subsidy, to see whether or not a similar picture emerges.

Limiting eligibility for housing benefit

In our latest survey we asked respondents to:

Consider a working age couple on a low income who receive money from the government to help them pay their rent. They have more bedrooms than the government thinks they need.

Do you think the amount of money they receive should or should not be reduced because of this?

As Figure 2 shows, there is much less support for the policy direction taken by the government on this issue then there is for limiting eligibility for unemployment benefit. While 4 in 10 (40%) think the amount of money a working-age couple receives in these circumstances should be reduced, suggesting they are potentially supportive of the government's approach, more than half (55%) do not think it should be reduced. Indeed, as many as a quarter are "definitely" opposed to the idea.

Given this question was asked for the first time in 2015, we cannot be sure whether support for the government's approach has risen or fallen since the policy was first introduced in April 2013. However, we might note that whereas the internet polling company, YouGov, found that 49% supported this policy in March 2013 (just before its implementation), by July 2014 (some fifteen months later) it had fallen to 41%.[4] While we cannot compare our BSA reading with these polls due to differences in sampling and question wording, it may be the case that the 40% who now support this aspect of welfare reform was rather higher in the past.

Figure 2 Views on reducing the money received from government by a working age couple with more bedrooms than they need

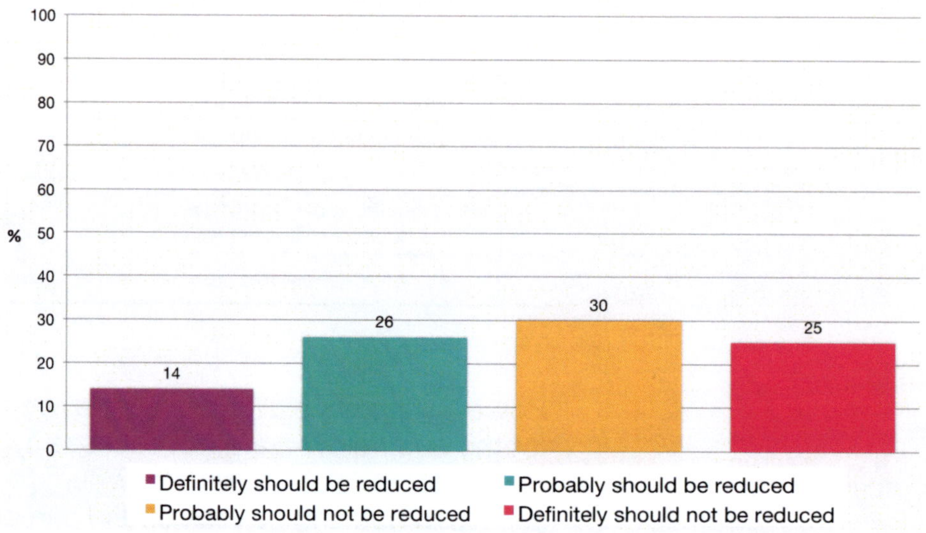

Unweighted base 3266

We have discovered that the public is rather more supportive of reducing the circumstances in which particular benefits can be received than they are of reducing spending on welfare. However, the substantial differences in attitudes to these two strands of reform, and to particular types of benefit and categories of recipient, implies that individuals' attitudes towards different aspects of welfare may be influenced by different considerations. It is to this question that we turn next.

The public is rather more supportive of reducing the circumstances in which particular benefits can be received than they are of reducing spending on welfare

4 https://yougov.co.uk/news/2014/07/18/bedroom-tax-divisive-ever/

Support for welfare reform: ideology or self-interest?

In the second part of this chapter, we consider the characteristics that appear to shape, on the one hand, attitudes towards levels of welfare spending and, on the other, attitudes towards tightening eligibility. In each case we focus on two measures. We consider what shapes attitudes towards overall levels of spending, by analysing our question on whether people agree or disagree that "the government should reduce spending on welfare benefits for the poor" and a question on one of specific topics that has recently generated political controversy, that is, whether people think that a working couple with children should "look after themselves ...as best they can", rather than have their wages topped up by the government. Meanwhile, so far as attitudes towards eligibility are concerned, we focus on who does and does not think that unemployment benefit should only be available for a limited period, and attitudes towards reducing the housing benefit of those deemed to have a spare room.

There are two broad sets of influences that we might think shape attitudes towards these topics. First of all, we might anticipate that someone's attitude towards welfare reform will be determined by their wider moral and political attitudes and values – such as the political party with which they identify and their general attitudes to the welfare state. So, for example, we might expect someone who is generally in favour of reducing government taxation and spending to want to see levels of welfare spending reduced. Equally, we might expect someone who is in favour of redistributing income to support increasing spending on welfare benefits for the poor and the topping up of the wages of low income families.

Alternatively, an individual's support for elements of welfare reform might be influenced by their personal circumstances. We might envisage that someone in receipt of a particular benefit would be less likely to support reforms that would result in spending on or eligibility for that benefit being reduced. Applying this logic more broadly, those in particular income or age groups might have views that reflect the interests of 'their' group. So we might anticipate that those with the lowest household incomes, who would be more likely to receive benefits, would be less supportive of welfare reform than those with the highest incomes. Equally, we might anticipate that older people are less supportive of working-age benefits from which they are unlikely to benefit, even though they may not necessarily mean that they are less supportive of welfare in general (Duffy, 2013).

Support for reducing spending on benefits

Table 5 shows how the level of disagreement with the proposition that welfare spending on the poor should increase varies according to a variety of ideological and demographic indicators. So far as ideological position is concerned, opposition to increasing welfare spending in general is higher among Conservative than among Labour supporters, among those who think that overall levels of taxation and spending should be reduced rather than increased,[5] and, most markedly, amongst those who oppose redistribution[6] as compared with those in favour. There are also some differences in the anticipated direction in respect of people's social background. Those on higher incomes, and those who (together with their partner) are not in receipt of benefits are more likely to oppose more welfare spending than are those on lower incomes and those who are receiving benefits. The differences are though rather smaller than they are in the case of our indicators of ideological position, while in fact there is no significant difference at all between the views of those in the youngest and oldest age groups.

Table 5 Attitudes towards reducing spending on welfare for the poor, by ideology and self-interest

	% disagree government should spend more on welfare benefits for poor	*Unweighted base*
All	31	*2781*
Measures of ideology		
Party identification		
Conservative	47	*957*
Labour	18	*757*
Attitude to government taxation and spending		
Should reduce taxes and spend less	45	*112*
Should increase taxes and spend more	17	*1307*
Attitude to redistribution		
Supports redistribution	19	*1200*
Opposes redistribution	56	*762*
Measures of self-interest		
Age group		
18-24	29	*186*
25-34	35	*381*
35-44	35	*457*
45-54	34	*493*
55-64	27	*487*
65-74	26	*468*
75+	26	*307*
Household income		
Highest quartile	39	*673*
Lowest quartile	22	*592*
Benefit receipt (respondent or partner)		
Receives any state benefit or tax credit	28	*1649*
Does not receive any state benefits or tax credits	35	*1127*

5 This is measured by a question that asked whether, if it had to choose, the government should 'reduce taxes and spend less on health, education and social benefits', keep taxation and spending 'at the same level as now', or increase taxes and spend more. For details of the pattern of response to this question see the chapter on politics.

6 Support for redistribution is measured by agreement with the statement "The government should redistribute income from the better-off to those who are less well-off".

However, these various indicators will often be related to each other. Conservative supporters are more likely to be opposed to more government spending and redistribution as well as being more likely to live in a high income household. To establish which of these indicators really are associated with attitudes towards the overall level of welfare spending, we need to use multivariate statistical analysis that identifies which indicators are significantly associated with attitudes towards welfare spending after bearing in mind not only the size of our sample, but also after controlling for the association between those attitudes and all of the other indicators we have taken into account. A summary of the result of such an analysis, in this instance a binary logistic regression, is shown in Table 6 (Model 1). [7]

This confirms much of the impression created by Table 5. It finds that not only age but also whether someone is in receipt of benefit is not significantly associated with opposition to spending more on welfare benefits. Meanwhile, although household income is still significant the association proves to be relatively weak. In contrast, all three measures of ideology remain significant and important predictors of attitudes. This means, for example, that even among Conservative supporters, opposition to increasing spending on welfare is even greater if someone is also opposed to redistribution of income and to more government taxation and spending. In any event it seems clear that attitudes to reducing spending on welfare benefits are primarily a reflection of ideology rather than self-interest.

7 Further details of the logistics regression analyses undertaken are available from the author on request.

Table 6 Results of multivariate analysis of characteristics which predict support for reducing spending on welfare

	Model 1	**Model 2**
	Disagree that government should spend more on welfare benefits for the poor	**Think that working age couple struggling to make ends meet should look after themselves**
Independent variables included in models		
Characteristics relating to ideology		
Party identification	+++	+++
Attitudes to welfare	not included[8]	+++
Attitudes to redistribution	+++	+++
Attitudes to taxation and spending	+++	
Characteristics relating to self-interest		
Age group		
Household income quartiles	+	+
Benefit receipt (for respondent and partner)[9]		+++
Whether respondent has any children in household	not included	+++

+++ = significant at 99% level
+ = significant at 95% level

However, the pattern we find for attitudes to the government topping up wages for a working couple with children is somewhat different (see Table 7). Here too, attitudes are linked to the three indicators of ideological position that we used previously. Those who support the Conservatives, who oppose redistribution and who want less taxation and government spending are all more likely to believe that the couple should make ends meet without government help. At the same time we can also see that someone who broadly has an outlook that can be categorised as anti-welfare[10] is also more likely to hold that view.

Just 14% of those currently in receipt of tax credits think that the couple should look after themselves, compared with 31% of those not in receipt of this benefit

On this topic, though, it appears that respondents' apparent self-interest also makes a difference. Most markedly, just 14% of those currently in receipt of tax credits think that the couple should look after themselves, compared with 31% of those not in receipt of this benefit. Equally older people, and those living in households without children are also more likely to feel that the couple should look after themselves. Evidently those who currently are benefitting from tax credits or who are of an age and a family situation whereby they might be potential beneficiaries take a rather different perspective on this subject than those who do not. This suggests that whatever

8 We did not include the welfarism scale (as outlined in fn. 9 below) in the analysis of disagreement with the view that the government should spend more on welfare benefits for the poor, as this is one of the eight questionnaire items on which the scale is based.

9 For Model 1, we compared the views of those respondents who reported that they or their spouse were receiving any of the state benefits asked about. For Model 2, we compared the views of those respondents receiving tax credits (Working Tax Credit and/or Child Tax Credit) with those not receiving any tax credits.

10 BSA includes a welfare scale based on eight agree-disagree items designed to measure broad attitudes to the welfare state and welfare recipients. The Technical Details contain further information regarding how the welfarism scale is constructed and validated.

may be the position in respect of attitudes towards welfare benefits in general, attitudes towards specific benefits reflect self-interest as well as ideological predisposition.

Table 7 Attitudes towards government topping up wages of low income childless couple, by Ideology and self-interest

	% oppose topping up wages of low income childless couple	*Unweighted base*
All	29	*2781*
Measures of ideology		
Party identification		
Conservative	46	*957*
Labour	18	*757*
Attitudes to welfare		
Pro-welfare	11	*681*
Anti-welfare	53	*445*
Attitude to government taxation and spending		
Should reduce taxes and spend less	36	*112*
Should increase taxes and spend more	24	*1307*
Attitude to redistribution		
Supports redistribution	20	*1200*
Opposes redistribution	45	*762*
Measures of self-interest		
Age group		
18-24	25	*186*
25-34	29	*381*
35-44	27	*457*
45-54	26	*493*
55-64	31	*487*
65-74	33	*468*
75+	37	*307*
Household income		
Highest quartile	34	*673*
Lowest quartile	21	*592*
Benefit receipt (respondent or partner)		
Receives any tax credits	14	*342*
Does not receive any tax credits	31	*2439*

This is confirmed by the results of a multivariate analysis (shown in Table 6 – Model 2). True, with the sole exception of attitudes to taxation and government spending, all of our measures of ideology remain significant predictors of attitudes to topping up wages, once the relationships between them are all controlled for. However, our measures of social and economic background play a more important role than they did in respect of attitudes towards the overall level of welfare spending. Being in receipt of a tax credit together with the presence of children in the household remain significant predictors of views on topping up wages even after taking into account people's ideological outlook, while household income is also significantly, if less importantly, associated with people's views.

Support for limiting the circumstances in which benefits can be received

But what about attitudes towards tightening eligibility for benefits? Once again ideological outlook appears to matter. As the left hand column of Table 8 shows, those who identify with the Conservative Party, those who are opposed to redistribution and those whose overall outlook is unsympathetic to welfare are markedly more likely to believe that unemployment benefit should only be paid for a limited period of time. For example, around four in five of those who can be regarded as anti-welfare believe that the length of time for which unemployment benefit is paid should be limited, compared with only around 3 in 10 of those whose attitude to welfare in general is relatively sympathetic. At the same time, however, those who are currently in receipt of unemployment benefit are also much less likely to support the idea than are those who are not in receipt of benefit.[11] Similarly, there are also less marked differences between those living in high and those in low income households, and between older and younger respondents.

11 Only 65 respondents to this question reported that they or their spouse was in receipt of unemployment benefit, so caution needs to be applied to this finding.

Table 8 Attitudes towards limiting length of time someone can claim Unemployment Benefit and paying Housing Benefit for spare rooms, by ideology and social background

	% support limiting duration of unemployment benefit	% support removing spare room subsidy	*Unweighted base*
All	60	40	*3266*
Measures of ideology			
Party identification			
Conservative	72	49	*1075*
Labour	48	32	*943*
Attitudes to welfare			
Pro-welfare	31	23	*681*
Anti-welfare	84	58	*445*
Attitude to government taxation and spending			
Should reduce taxes and spend less	56	54	*134*
Should increase taxes and spend more	55	33	*1505*
Attitude to redistribution			
Supports redistribution	49	33	*1200*
Opposes redistribution	71	46	*762*
Measures of self-interest			
Age group			
18-24	56	48	*228*
25-34	57	47	*479*
35-44	63	45	*555*
45-54	57	38	*567*
55-64	58	31	*546*
65-74	65	32	*514*
75+	64	31	*373*
Household income			
Highest quartile	64	45	*742*
Lowest quartile	50	35	*691*
Benefit receipt (respondent or partner)			
Receives unemployment benefit	24	not included	*65*
Does not receive unemployment benefit	60	not included	*3201*
Receives housing benefit	not included	29	*400*
Does not receive housing benefit	not included	41	*2866*

With the exception of benefit receipt, all of these measures continue to be associated with attitudes towards limiting the duration of unemployment benefit when we include them in a multivariate analysis (see Table 9, Model 3). In this instance then, it appears that once again support for limiting eligibility for benefits is driven both by ideology and by apparent self-interest.

Table 9 Results of multivariate analysis of characteristics which predict support for limiting circumstances in which benefits can be received

	Model 3	**Model 4**
	Agree that duration of unemployment benefit should be limited	**Support idea of working age couple with too many bedrooms giving some of benefit back to govt**
Independent variables included in models		
Characteristics relating to ideology		
Party identification	+	+++
Attitudes to welfare	+++	+++
Attitudes to redistribution	+++	
Attitudes to taxation and spending		+++
Characteristics relating to self-interest		
Age group	+++	+++
Household income quartiles	+++	
Currently in receipt of benefit (respondent and/or partner)		

+++ = *significant at 99% level*

\+ = *significant at 95% level*

Younger people are less likely to oppose topping up the wages of a low income couple and limiting the duration of unemployment benefit. However, they prove to be more likely to back cutting the housing benefit of those who have a spare room

Much the same also appears to be true of attitudes towards the spare room subsidy (Table 8, right hand column). Again Conservative supporters and those who can be regarded as anti-welfare are more likely to support cutting the housing benefit of those who are of working age and are deemed to have more bedrooms than they need. This is also the case for those who are in favour of a reduction in taxation and government spending. At the same time so also are those who live in a high income household and who are not themselves in receipt of housing benefit. But there is also one key difference between the pattern of attitudes towards this subject and what we have otherwise observed so far. Hitherto we have found that younger people are less likely to oppose topping up the wages of a low income couple and limiting the duration of unemployment benefit. However, they prove to be more likely to back cutting the housing benefit of those who have a spare room. Most likely, this reflects the fact that, on this subject, the self-interest of younger people would appear to be in tune with the government's reform. Younger people who are struggling to find somewhere to live, or at least somewhere big enough to live, may well feel that older people who are occupying properties that are bigger than their needs following the departure of their children from the family home should be encouraged to downsize to a smaller property. Indeed, when we take a multivariate analysis (Table 9, Model 4), we find that age continues to be significantly associated with attitudes towards the spare room subsidy, alongside, once again, people's ideological outlook.

The overall picture

Ideology evidently plays an important role in shaping attitudes towards welfare. This is true whether we are looking at attitudes towards the level of welfare spending in general or at attitudes towards specific benefits. In contrast, for the most part apparent self-interest does not play much of a role in influencing attitudes towards the level of welfare spending as a whole, but can make a difference when it comes to specific benefits. Moreover, this can mean that the attitudes of those in different social groups can vary depending on the benefit in question. In particular, while younger people appear more sympathetic to tax credits and unemployment benefit, for which they might potentially be eligible, they are less keen on continuing to pay housing benefit to those deemed to have a spare room, a position in which they are less likely to find themselves. Thus although for the most part attitudes towards the government's welfare programme will reflect voters' broad ideological outlook, irrespective of the benefit in question, they may also be influenced by a perceived self-interest that means that some reforms are more or less popular with particular groups than others.

Conclusions

While public opinion has begun to shift in relation to spending on retirement pensions, it certainly is not the case that the government's protection of spending on benefits for pensioners has generated a backlash in public opinion

Our evidence suggests that it is perhaps not surprising that on occasion the government's programme of welfare reform has aroused controversy. It seems that only a minority back the overall objective of reducing levels of spending on welfare. Meanwhile, it appears that many would like to see an increase in the benefits paid to some recipients of welfare, most notably, carers, people with disabilities and those on low incomes who have children. Attempts to cut or curb welfare for these groups seem destined to hit choppy waters, as indeed has proven to be the case. Yet, while public opinion has begun to shift in relation to spending on retirement pensions, it certainly is not the case that the government's protection of spending on benefits for pensioners has generated a backlash in public opinion; the public remain relatively favourable towards spending on this group.

But there are other groups to whom the public are much less sympathetic, including above all, the unemployed. There is widespread support for having tight eligibility rules for unemployment benefit and a belief that people should be finding another job as soon as possible, rather than seeking one that they would like to do. Meanwhile, far from being universally unpopular, the question of cutting the housing benefit of those with a spare room divides public opinion, including not least younger and older people. More generally, curbing eligibility for benefits appears to be rather more palatable to the public than cutting levels of benefit, although those most affected by any such curb are always likely to object the most irrespective of whether they are more generally in favour of cutting welfare expenditure. The issue looks set to continue to be a political minefield.

References

Conservative Party (2010), *Invitation to join the government of Britain: Conservative manifesto, 2010*, available at: https://www.conservatives.com/~/media/files/activist%20centre/press%20and%20policy/manifestos/manifesto2010

Conservative Party (2015), *Manifesto*, available at: https://www.conservatives.com/manifesto

Department for Work and Pensions (2013), *Public perceptions of the removal of the spare room subsidy (RSRS),* available at: https://www.gov.uk/government/uploads/system/uploads/attachment_data/file/255654/public-perceptions-of-rsrs.pdf

Duffy, B., Hall, S., O'Leary, D. and Pope, S. (2013) *Generation strains: a Demos and Ipsos-MORI report on changing attitudes to welfare*

H. M. Treasury (2010), *Budget 2010*, available at https://www.gov.uk/government/uploads/system/uploads/attachment_data/file/248096/0061.pdf

H. M. Treasury (2013), *Spending review 2010*, available at: https://www.gov.uk/government/publications/spending-review-2010

Hood, A. and Phillips, D. (2015), *Benefit spending and reforms: the coalition government's record,* Institute for Fiscal Studies:, IFS briefing note BN160, election briefing note 2015 No. 3, ISBN: 978-1-909463-74-5

Taylor-Gooby, P. and Taylor, E. (2015), 'Benefits and welfare: long-term trends or short term reactions?', in Curtice, J. and Ormston, R. *British Social Attitudes; the 32nd report*, available at: http://www.bsa.natcen.ac.uk/latest-report/british-social-attitudes-32/welfare.aspx

The Coalition (2010), *Our Programme for Government*, available at: https://www.gov.uk/government/uploads/system/uploads/attachment_data/file/78977/coalition_programme_for_government.pdf

Acknowledgements

NatCen Social Research would like to thank the Department for Work and Pensions for funding some of the questions reported in this chapter. The views expressed here are those of the author alone.

Appendix

The data for Figure 1 are shown below.

Table A.1 Attitudes to welfare benefits, 1987–2015

	1987	1989	1991	1993	1994	1995	1996	1998	1999	2000
% disagree government should spend more money on welfare benefits	22	15	17	20	23	23	26	26	28	30
Unweighted base	*1281*	*2604*	*2481*	*2567*	*2929*	*3135*	*3103*	*3000*	*2450*	*2980*

	2001	2002	2003	2004	2005	2006	2007	2008	2009	2010
% disagree government should spend more money on welfare benefits	26	26	26	32	31	29	33	35	43	39
Unweighted base	*2795*	*2900*	*873*	*2609*	*2699*	*2822*	*2672*	*3000*	*967*	*2810*

	2011	2012	2013	2014	2015
% disagree government should spend more money on welfare benefits	39	32	32	39	31
Unweighted base	*2841*	*2855*	*2832*	*2376*	*2754*

Work

Attitudes and experiences of work in a changing labour market

The labour market has seen various changes since the 1980s, with greater numbers now in employment, and a higher proportion of graduates in the population as a whole. The UK is still recovering from the financial crisis of 2008 and the recession that followed. Against this backdrop of a shifting labour market, our chapter asks how attitudes to work, and experiences of it, have changed.

More have good quality jobs, though job security remains elusive for some

71% of workers have a 'good' job (one with at least 4 positive attributes such as being interesting, helping others and/or society, and offering chances for advancement), compared with 62% in 2005 and 57% in 1989.

Think job security is important

Think they have job security

While 92% of people think that job security is either important, or very important, only around two-thirds of workers (65%) agree they actually have this in their job.

Jobs are valued beyond their financial benefits

62% of respondents say they would enjoy having a job even if they didn't need the money, up from 49% in 2005.

Social class and education make a difference to financial motivations to work; 63% of those in professional or managerial occupations disagree a job is solely about the money earned, while the same is true for only 34% of those in routine or semi-routine occupations.

Stress at work has increased

37% of workers experience stress "always" or "often", compared with 28% in 1989. Professional and managerial workers, and those aged 35-44 are most likely to feel stressed.

Author

Stephen McKay, University of Lincoln
Ian Simpson, Senior Researcher, NatCen Social Research

Introduction

For many people under the age of 65, work is a central feature of life. The quality of a person's job can have an important bearing on their health and life chances (Coats and Lehki, 2008). Jobs associated with better health and wellbeing include those with more autonomy, security and good financial rewards (Bryson et al., 2011). In recent years, academic and popular attention has focused on two changes in the labour market that have raised concerns about the prevalence of poor quality jobs and the negative impact of the changing nature of some jobs. First is the possibility that the labour market is 'polarising', meaning that there are more good jobs, and more bad jobs, with a hollowing out of middling jobs in between (Goos and Manning, 2007). Second is the notion of 'work intensification' – the idea that, despite higher living standards, more is now demanded of workers in terms of shorter deadlines, a faster pace of work, potentially greater monitoring of individuals, and overall a higher level of stress (Green, 2007). This may overlap with issues of polarisation if only some groups of workers are facing such harsher working conditions.

Questions and concerns about the quality of a person's job may seem less vital at a time when the real pressure is on having a job at all. As we write, the UK continues to slowly emerge from a deep and prolonged period of recession. Many jobs were lost at the start of that recession, but fewer than would have been expected given the reduction in the overall level of economic activity (McKay and Smith, 2015). A longer-term perspective reveals that employment levels are actually higher now than in the 1980s. But the recession has a broader impact than employment rates alone. Wage growth has remained very slow, trailing behind changes in prices in many years after the recession. By 2015 (when the latest survey took place), wages had started to rise, and employment continued on a strong upward path. Despite this, levels of optimism about the recovery and any growth in living standards have, if anything, tended to stall.

How do these theories about the changing nature of work and labour market trends relate to people's attitudes to and experiences of work? This chapter uses long-term data on work orientation and perceptions of job quality to explore a number of related questions. We begin by asking how attitudes to work have changed over the longer-term, and whether there's any evidence of the impact of the recession. We then examine the extent to which people have the type of jobs that they want, and assess whether jobs are polarising (with evidence of both more good jobs *and* more bad jobs over time). Finally we look at how stressed workers are feeling and how much control or autonomy they have in their jobs, to shed light on whether work has intensified over time. Throughout, we consider whether different subgroups (using a range of socio-demographic background characteristics) have particular work attitudes and experiences.

Our chapter draws on data from a module of questions on Work Orientation, included in the survey as part of the International Social Survey Programme (ISSP). The questions have been fielded four times, in 1989, 1997, 2005 and 2015, allowing us to examine long-term trends in people's attitudes towards, and experiences of, work. The timing of the two most recent readings limits the potential of the data to reveal *short-term* responses to the recession - 2005 being before it occurred, and 2015 being a relatively optimistic moment of the recovery from the recession. We will however reflect on whether there are any signs of a *lasting* impact of the recession on attitudes to work.

Setting the scene: labour market trends

We start by reviewing some overarching trends in the labour market. In 2015, 56% of people overall are in work - a rather higher proportion than in the early 1980s and mid-1990s (see Figure 1), with actual numbers in work reaching record levels (ONS, 2016). While the recession of the early 1990s was rather less severe than that of the most recent global financial crash (Faccini and Hackworth, 2010), its effect on rates of employment was rather greater. In contrast, since 2008/09, the overall proportion in work has been fairly consistent, with rates stable for those aged 40-59, and increasing somewhat for those aged 60 or older (rates are now around four percentage points higher than the years prior to the crisis).

It is younger people who have faced the greatest challenges in remaining in, or securing, paid work

It is younger people who have faced the greatest challenges in remaining in, or securing, paid work. In 2015, 65% of people aged under 40 were in paid work, compared with 78% of those aged 40-59. For the under 40s, this is a level similar to most years since 2010, lower than the 70% figure seen in most years in the preceding decade. The figure also illustrates the differential experiences of younger and older workers. The employment rates of these groups had been converging in the early 2000s, but since then a gap has opened up which shows no sign of closing. This may be due to employers restricting recruitment during the recession and the subsequent slow recovery, particularly affecting those new to the labour market.

Figure 1 Percentage in paid work, by age, 1984-2015

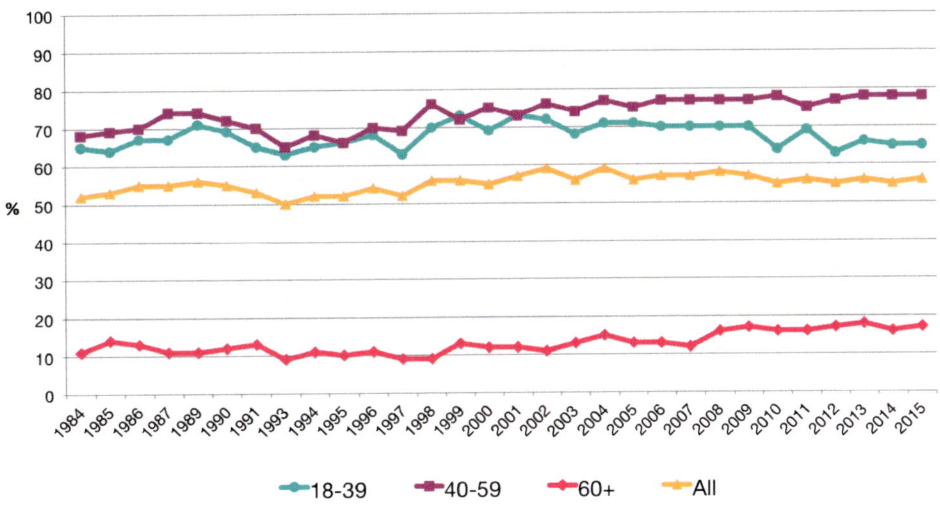

Base: all
The data on which Figure 1 is based can be found in the appendix to this chapter

One of the other notable changes in the available workforce in recent decades is the rising number of graduates, following the continued expansion of higher education. During the three decades covered by the British Social Attitudes survey series, the proportion of people with a degree-level qualification has risen sharply from 10% in 1984 to 24% now. This change has affected all age groups, though the pace of growth has understandably been slower among those aged 60 or older, but even for this age group the proportion of graduates has risen from 5% to 15% over the same period. For those aged 18-39, the proportion of graduates has increased from 14% to 30%, while for those aged 40-59 the equivalent figures are 10% increasing to 26%. This change has a bearing on the nature of the labour market, as graduates tend to command higher wages, a premium maintained despite the growth in their numbers. They are also more likely to have professional careers: in 2015, 72% of working graduates have a professional or managerial occupation, compared with 45% of all in work.

The proportion of people with a degree-level qualification has risen sharply from 10% in 1984 to 24% now

Over time, participation rates of women have increased relative to men. So, looking at those aged from 18 to 59 in 1984 some 74% of men were in paid work compared with 60% of women. By 2015 the rates were 77% for men and 67% for women. The pay gap between men and women has also reduced over time but remains significant, with the difference in median full-time hourly earnings still 9.4% in the latest data (from the 2015 Annual Survey of Hours and Earnings) compared with 17.4% in 1997. So, there has been a degree of convergence but large differences still remain.

The distribution of objective social class (a measure of occupational status, based on the type of job someone has – or their last job if not currently working) has also changed over time. This transformation is well documented, and associated with the decline in employment in the British manufacturing industry over the last few decades (Lindsay, 2003). Latest data from ONS show that in 2016, 22% of people in work are in semi-routine or routine jobs.[1]

These four key socio-demographic variables - age, sex, education and social class - are themselves associated with people's experience of, or relationship with, the labour market. They are related not just to employment rates, but also the types of jobs, level of pay, hours worked and so on, that people have (see ONS, 2016 for recent labour market analyses). In the rest of the chapter, we therefore note where these characteristics are related to attitudes towards, and experiences of, paid work.

Figure 2 shows some other key trends in the labour market over time (using other data sources). First, the proportion that are members of a trade union is in long-term decline. In 1984 close to 11 million workers were members of trade unions, but this has dropped to a little over 6 million by 2015. This trend may help to explain changes in income inequality, which in turn is driven by changes in wages (and in social security benefits). Conditions in the lower half of the income distribution seem to be strongly linked to the decline of unionisation for lower-skilled jobs (Holmes and Mayhew, 2012). However the declines in union coverage were most marked during the late 1980s and early 1990s, when inequality was increasing, and since the late 1980s reductions in coverage have occurred but at a more gradual rate.

Conversely, the proportion working in the public sector increased between 1999 (when consistent data was first available) and 2009, rising from 5.4 million jobs to 6.3 million. Since then numbers have decreased to 5.4 million, the lowest since 1999.[2]

Self-employment now represents 4.5 million workers

Last, we note that self-employment has been rising over the last 15 or so years, and now represents 4.5 million workers. While employment did not fall proportionately in the years after the 2008 financial crisis, many of the new jobs created (at least for a time) tended to be part-time or self-employed (Rowlingson and McKay, 2015). Self-employment may be portrayed positively as a sign of flexibility and an entrepreneurial spirit. However, some people may feel compelled to enter self-employment if more standard employment is not available, and often the self-employed find it harder to access pensions and other key benefits of employment. In a detailed analysis, D'Arcy and Gardiner (2014) tended to find more

1 This figure is based on NS-SEC (Socio-Economic Classification) and the data are available at www.ons.gov.uk/employmentandlabourmarket/peopleinwork/employmentandemployeetypes/datasets/. This is backed up by analysis of BSA data over time: in the 1989 survey, 25% were in the highest social class, while 37% were in the lowest social class. By 2015 the proportions have reversed: 43% are now in the highest social class while 22% are in the lowest class. Percentages are based on all those who have ever had a paid job. This excludes a small proportion of respondents who have never worked. The 1989 figures are based on a recoding of the Goldthorpe-Heath 5-category class scheme, while 2015 figures are based on a 5 category version of SEG (Socio-Economic Group) (as this results in categories which are conceptually similar over time). See footnote 5 for more detail on social class analysis in the rest of the chapter.

2 This ONS series allows for changes in the treatment of different groups as being in the public sector, for details see: http://www.ons.gov.uk/employmentandlabourmarket/peopleinwork/publicsectorpersonnel/bulletins/publicsectoremployment/december2015

reasons for concern than for celebration at this rising tide of self-employment, in particular owing to reduced earnings compared with employees.

Figure 2 Labour market trends - self-employment, trade unions and the public sector, 1984-2015 (thousands)

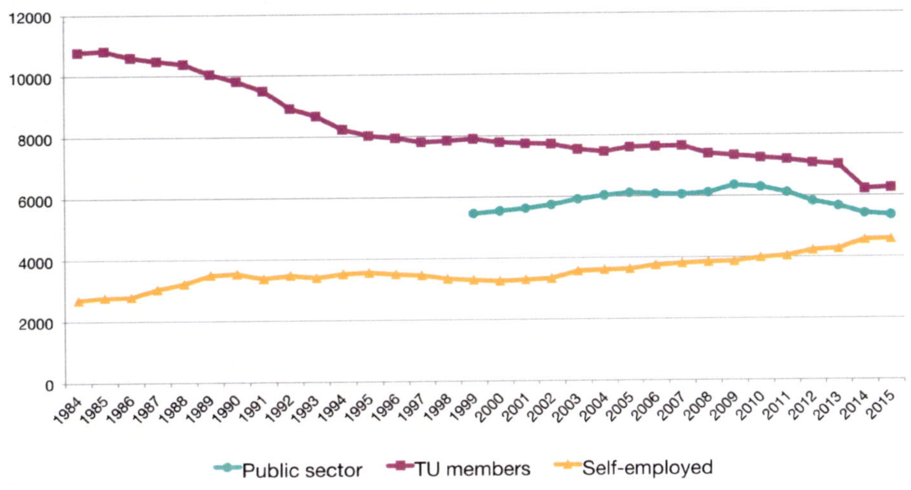

Source: Labour Force Survey (self-employment data), ONS Public Sector Employment series, BIS (trade union membership)[3]
The data on which Figure 2 is based can be found in the appendix to this chapter

Attitudes to work

We start our examination of the ISSP data by looking at overall attitudes to work, including job satisfaction and financial motivations. In the years after a recession one might expect job satisfaction to increase, as people are grateful to be in any job (see trends in Donegani et al., 2012). In terms of work orientation, the extrinsic rewards of work may become more central when there is pressure on public and private finances.

Overall job satisfaction is at the same level as in 2005

At regular intervals we have asked workers "How satisfied are you with your main job?" In 2015, 14% are "completely satisfied" with their jobs, while 29% are "very satisfied" and 38% "fairly". There is no evidence of a sustained increase in satisfaction during the last recession. Overall job satisfaction is at the same level as in 2005, when the recession was still some way off (and largely unanticipated), when 15% were "completely satisfied", 27% "very satisfied" and 38% "fairly satisfied". There has been a small increase over the longer-term, with satisfaction somewhat higher now than in 1997, when the economy had been growing for some years, (when 13% were "completely satisfied" and 22% "very satisfied").

The gap between our two most recent data points means we cannot

3 Relevant sources are: for LFS self-employment data: http://www.ons.gov.uk/employmentandlabourmarket/peopleinwork/employmentandemployeetypes/timeseries/dyzn; for public sector employment: http://www.ons.gov.uk/employmentandlabourmarket/peopleinwork/publicsectorpersonnel/bulletins/publicsectoremployment/march2016; and, for trades union membership: https://www.gov.uk/government/statistics/trade-union-statistics-2015

rule out a (short-lived) increase in the years immediately following the 2008 financial crisis. Indeed there is evidence of that from other sources; McManus and Perry writing in our 29th Report (2012) found job satisfaction had increased in the first few years after the crisis, albeit using a different measure.

What of our assumption that the experience of recession might have strengthened financial motivations to work? We asked all respondents (not just those in work) how far they agree or disagree with the following statements:

> ***I would enjoy having a paid job even if I did not need the money***
>
> ***A job is just a way of earning money - no more***

62% of people say they would enjoy having a job even if they didn't need the money

Is work all about the money? It seems not. A majority say they would enjoy working even if they didn't need the money - and this proportion has been slowly increasing over time (see Table 1). In 2015, 62% of people say they would enjoy having a job even if they didn't need the money, up from 49% in each of 2005 and 1997, and 54% in 1989. Twice as many in 2015, compared with 1989, *strongly* agree that they would enjoy having employment even if their financial circumstances did not require it.

Similarly, around half disagree that "a job is just a way of earning money", and nothing more (with smaller proportions agreeing), and on this measure there has been little change over time. Taken together, this somewhat weak financial motivation to work is reinforced by findings later in the chapter which show that people in work do not rate having a high income as being especially important, particularly when compared with greater job security and having an interesting job.

Table 1 Financial motivation to work, 1989-2015

	1989	1997	2005	2015
Would enjoy having a job even if didn't need the money				
% Strongly agree	7	6	9	14
% Agree	47	42	40	48
A job is just a way of earning money - no more				
% Disagree	39	35	35	34
% Strongly disagree	13	11	12	15
Unweighted base	*1516*	*1080*	*913*	*1793*

Base: all

Slightly more of those in professional occupations, and graduates, say they would work even if they did not need the income, but differences are relatively small. However, on the second question

65% of graduates disagree that a job is only about earning money, compared with just 35% of those with no qualifications

(which is the far stronger statement about a job being solely about money) there are large differences by social class and education. In 2015, 63% of those in professional or managerial occupations disagree that a job is solely about the money earned compared with only 34% of those in routine or semi-routine occupations (and 49% overall). There has been little change on this since 2005. A similar pattern is evident for education, with 65% of graduates disagreeing that a job is only about earning money, compared with 48% of those with O level/GCSE qualifications and just 35% of those with no qualifications. There are only small, or no differences in financial motivation by age and by sex.

What people want - and get - from their jobs

We turn now to look at people's views about which different attributes they think are important in a job, and - for those in work - which of these they have in their employment. A number of these questions have been consistently asked since our survey began, which permits analysis of changes in the nature of people's relationship with the labour market over time. First, we gave respondents a list of different job attributes, and asked them to say how important they personally thought each one was:

Job security

High income

Good opportunities for advancement

An interesting job

A job that allows someone to work independently

A job that allows someone to help other people

A job that is useful to society

A job that allows someone to decide their times or days of work

A job that involves personal contact with other people

Job security is regarded as important by almost all (92%)

Figure 3 shows features of jobs regarded as important to varying degrees by respondents, ranked in order of importance. Clearly people regard many features of jobs as being "important", or indeed "very important". Job security is regarded as important by almost all (92%), while a majority say it is "very important" (57%), the only attribute for which this was true. Next most highly rated in terms of significance is having an interesting job, which 45% regard as "very important", while a further 45% say that it is "important". Other features rated particularly important are: having good opportunities for advancement, and having a job that is helpful to others and/or useful to society. One feature that relatively few (13%) see as "very important" is having a high income, although half (51%) do think this is at least "important".

There are some modest differences between men and women in the kinds of attributes they think are important in any job. Women are more likely to emphasise a job that involves helping other people (25% say that is "very important", compared with 17% of men), and involves personal contact with others (23% of women rate that "very important", 16% of men). Women also place a little more emphasis on being able to decide which days were worked, or which times (12% see that as "very important", compared with 8% of men), perhaps reflecting the fact that women are more likely than men to be working 'flexibly'.

Figure 3 Perceived importance of different job attributes

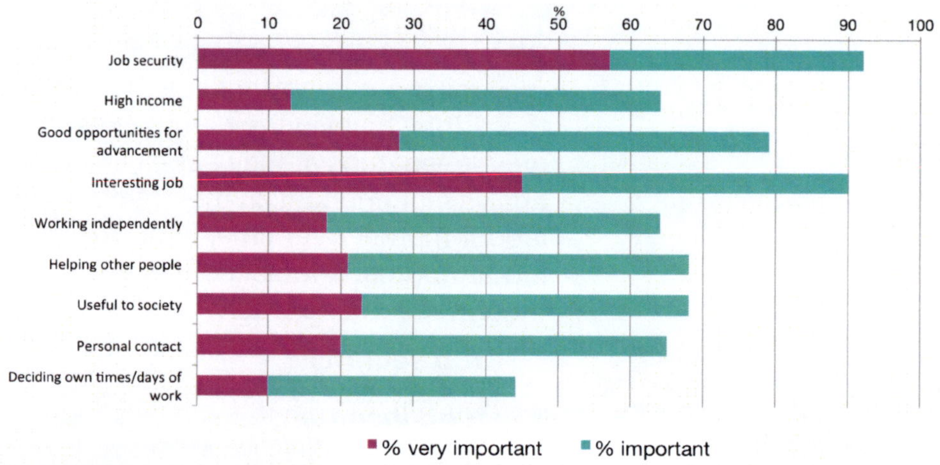

Base: all
The data on which Figure 3 is based can be found in the appendix to this chapter

We then asked those currently in work whether or not they felt their jobs actually had these characteristics, regardless of whether they felt they were important or not. In Figure 4 we plot the different job characteristics showing how people assessed them both in terms of whether they think they are important facets of a job (i.e. "important" or "very important"), and whether they actually have them (either agreeing or strongly agreeing that these statements apply to their job).[4] For this chart, the analysis is restricted only to those in paid work.

This chart enables us to see directly which attributes are important but not achieved, or which are generally achieved but seen as being of less importance. Those plotted below the x=y line are regarded as important, but workers are less likely to say that their jobs have these characteristics. Prominent among these are job security, good opportunities for advancement, and having an interesting job. Having a high income is also regarded as important by many workers, but fewer say their incomes are high - though this is quite a common feature of self-reporting incomes and not specific to labour market

4 The questions about whether jobs have these features very closely mirror the questions asked about the importance of those features, though not the question regarding how working times are decided (so this is excluded).

Improvements in the area of job security would probably be most appreciated by those in paid work

issues. This chart implies that improvements in the area of job security would probably be most appreciated by those in paid work, while changes to generate more interesting jobs - or make jobs more interesting - would also be beneficial. Workers are also unlikely to say that they have good opportunities for advancement in their current roles, despite regarding this as an important feature of a job.

Turning to the upper left half of the chart, many people have jobs that permit a high degree of contact with others, and independence about working practices - somewhat higher than the proportions saying that such features are important. Having jobs that are capable of helping others directly, or being of help to wider society, are also quite commonly attained in practice, and mirror the proportions rating these as important facets of any job.

Figure 4 Perceived importance of different job attributes, and whether workers have these in their jobs

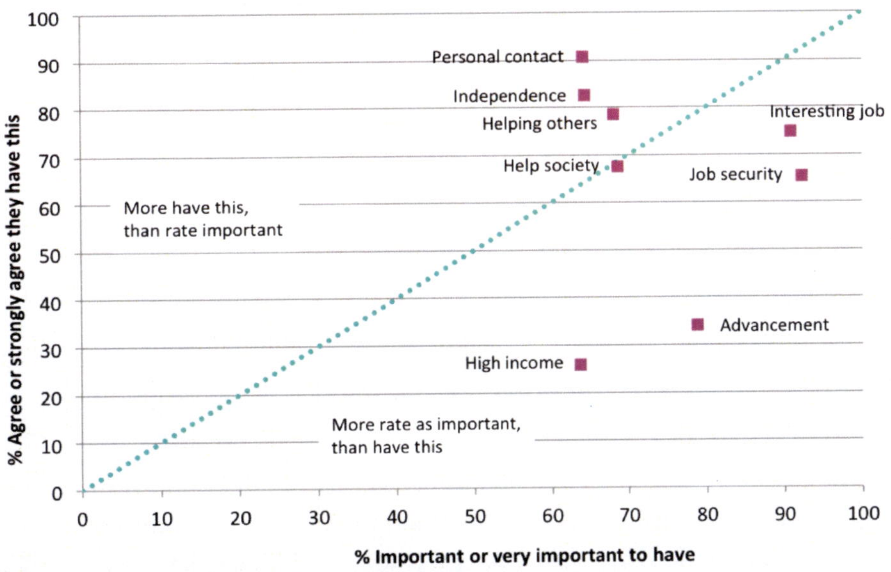

Base: all in work
The data on which Figure 4 is based can be found in the appendix to this chapter

Are jobs polarising?

Proponents of this theory say that the labour market has been 'polarising' since the 1980s, resulting in more good jobs, and more bad jobs, with a hollowing out of middling jobs in between (Goos and Manning, 2007). Supporting evidence is often produced that looks at skill levels or occupational grades, with the expectation that these are associated with terms and conditions of employment. It is suggested that technological changes and globalisation have removed many middle-rank jobs within manufacturing and more routine service functions. As a result work has been moved to lower-cost countries, or workers have been replaced by robots and/or IT. At the same time, higher skilled workers have been in greater demand, and more people have graduate level qualifications and are looking for such roles. Meanwhile, there seems to have been a growth in lower level service jobs, partly to meet the needs of the more highly paid. However, this view is not universally accepted (Anderson, 2009), or is accepted with regard to occupations perhaps but not to other labour market features (Plunkett and Paulo Pessoa, 2013). Our data provide an opportunity to investigate some longer-term evidence on this point, especially the lived experience of jobs of different kinds.

In order to assess whether jobs are polarising, we need to consider how the quality of jobs has changed over time. We measure the quality of jobs using the same seven characteristics reported above. These questions were included in a number of surveys separated by almost thirty years, and cover job security, high incomes, opportunities for advancement, whether jobs help people, or are useful to society, whether they are interesting, and allow for independence. We want to see to what extent the responses change over time - and for which groups they have changed the most.

We present these data in two different ways. First, we created an 'average' score for each attribute. To do this we recoded the responses so that those who agree they have the attribute are given a higher value, while those who disagree have a lower value, on a scale of one to five. This approach takes into account changes across all response categories: positive, neutral and negative. This is useful because in order to look for evidence of more bad jobs (as well as more good), if we focus only on the proportion who say they have a particular job attribute, it could give a misleading implication about the proportion who do not. For example, if the proportion who say they have a high income has increased, that does not necessarily imply a decrease in the proportion who do not (it could be that both have increased, with a reduction in the neutral middle category).

For most individual job attributes, workers are more likely now than in previous years to report having them

We plot how these aspects have changed over time in Figure 5. After taking account of positive, negative and neutral responses to the questions (by using our score), it is clear that for most individual job attributes, workers are more likely now than in previous years to report having them. They are more likely to say that their jobs are interesting, or useful to society, or have a high income, and so on, in 2015 compared with previous survey years. The one exception is job security, where there has been no increase in the last decade, but even so, those in work are more likely to say that their job is secure in 2015 than they were in either 1997 or 1989.

Figure 5 Whether workers have different job attributes (on a score from 1-5), 1989, 1997, 2005 and 2015

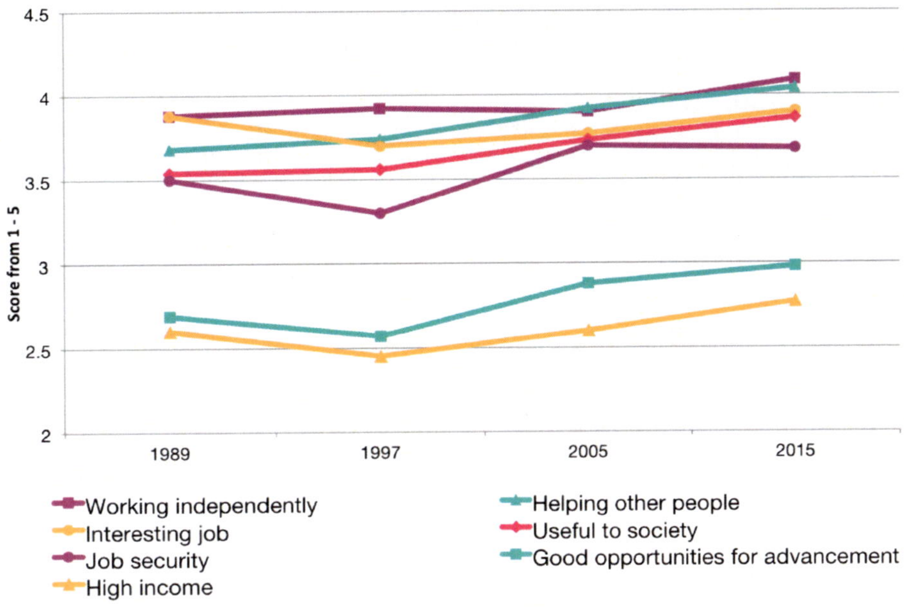

Note left-hand axis starts at value 2
Scores coded from 1-5, based on agree/neither/disagree response categories (don't knows excluded)
Base: all in work
The data on which Figure 5 is based can be found in the appendix to this chapter

There are some limitations to this analysis however. First, the polarisation view relates to the distribution of good and bad jobs, meaning that the overall average (presented above for different attributes) may not reveal any increase in the proportion with 'bad' jobs. Second, it is possible that the aggregate level findings may 'hide' increases in poor quality jobs for particular groups of workers, especially if good jobs outnumber bad, or if the former have also been increasing.

For that reason, we present two further analyses of these data. First, we look specifically at changes in job security, as this is the one attribute that has not increased in the last decade, and is highly valued. Have particular groups seen their jobs become less secure, as predicted by the 'job polarisation' view of the labour market? In Table 2 we show levels of job security, by age group and social class. Comparing the data for 2015 with 2005, we can see there is some indication that certain groups have fared disproportionately badly. The proportion with a secure job has fallen for those in the lowest social class, and for older workers - while younger workers have seen increases (though small sample sizes mean that changes are not significant for all age groups). This might be evidence of polarisation, as some groups have experienced an increase (or little change) in job security while other groups have had a decrease. Despite these changes over time, in 2015 social class is not significantly related to job security. What is clear is that while age was not significantly related to job security in 2005, the changes since have resulted in

Younger workers are now considerably more likely feel they have job security than their older counterparts

large gaps for workers of different ages. Younger workers are now considerably more likely feel they have job security than their older counterparts (this is true for 77% of 18-34 year olds versus 53% of 55-64 year olds).

Table 2 Job security at work, by age and social class, 2005 and 2015

% agree have job security	2005	2015	Change	*Unweighted base 2005*	*Unweighted base 2015*
All	66	65	-1	*502*	*942*
Age					
18-34	73	77	+4	*152*	*256*
35-44	62	70	+8	*133*	*223*
45-54	59	54	-5	*117*	*260*
55-64	67	53	-14	*86*	*164*
Social class					
Professional & managerial	65	67	+2	*221*	*444*
Semi-routine & routine	71	60	-11	*116*	*195*

Base: all in work

However the polarisation thesis is about the number of good and bad jobs overall, rather than changes on any one particular characteristic. To test this theory explicitly, we need to look at overall job quality, and to compare this for different subgroups, to see whether there are some groups of workers who have seen a decrease in job quality, even if overall there has been an increase. To do this, we look at a broader measure of job quality, which combines these different attributes into a score (from 0 to 7), based on the number of attributes the respondent reports having in their job. A low score implies a poor quality job, while a high score suggests a good quality job. For our analysis we have used a cut off of 4 attributes or more to mean a 'good' job, while 3 or less equates to a 'bad' job.

The overall proportion of workers with a good job has increased, from 57% in 1989 to 71% now

As Table 3 shows, the overall proportion of workers with a good job has increased, from 57% in 1989 to 71% now. When we look across a number of different socio-demographic characteristics, we find no evidence of polarisation; none of these subgroups have seen a decrease in job quality over the same period: younger and older workers, those in the highest and lowest social classes, and both men and women. True, there are still gaps between different groups, most notably when it comes to social class, where only just over 6 in 10 in the lowest social class have a 'good' job (using this definition), compared with a little under 8 in 10 in the highest social class. But even here, the gap has reduced over time, meaning that - on this measure and for these groups - there is no evidence of the labour market polarising in terms of jobs with desirable features.

Table 3 Proportion with 4 or more positive job attributes, by age and social class, 1989 and 2015

% with 4+ good job attributes	1989	2015	Change	*Unweighted base 1989*	*Unweighted base 2015*
All	57	71	+14	*720*	*942*
Age					
18-34	58	69	+14	*260*	*256*
35-44	55	79	+24	*200*	*223*
45-54	62	70	+8	*191*	*260*
55-64	48	63	+16	*75*	*164*
Social class[5]					
Highest social class (salariat)	72	77	+5	*224*	*465*
Lowest social class (working class)	42	62	+20	*216*	*160*

Base: all in work

In 2015, 69% of male workers and 73% of female workers have a 'good' job

Finally it is worth noting that using this definition there is no gap in job quality between male and female workers. In 2015, 69% of male workers and 73% of female workers have a 'good' job (the apparent small gap is not significant), an increase since 1989, when the proportion for both groups was around 57%.

Is work becoming more intensive?

We saw in the previous section that there have been various changes (mainly improvements) in the proportion who have 'good' jobs, and that there is no evidence in our data of jobs polarising. But there are other aspects of work that can have detrimental impacts on workers, even if other positive attributes are in place. We turn now to look at some of these other features of work, in order to assess the theory that work has become harder, or more intensive. To do this we look at changes over time in a range of different features of working life, including perceptions of stress, working hard, and the degree of autonomy and control that workers feel they have. If there has been work intensification we would expect to find more negative responses over time (more stress, working harder, less autonomy and control), with the latter two linked to debates about the extent to which employees are routinely monitored in terms of their work performance.

In 2015, 37% say that they find their work stressful

First, we asked "how often do you find your work stressful?" There has been something of an increase in levels of stress experienced by workers. In 2015, 37% say that they find their work stressful, either "always" or "often". This is a rise on both 1997 and 2005, when only 32% said the same, and compared with 1989 when the equivalent figure was 28%. These findings could be reflecting a degree of work intensification.

5 In Table 3, social class analysis for 1989 is based on a recoding of the Goldthorpe-Heath 5-category class scheme, while 2015 is based on a 5-category version of SEG (Socio-Economic Group) (as this results in categories which are conceptually similar over time). Elsewhere in the chapter, social class analyses for 2005 and 2015 use a five category version of the National Statistics Socio-Economic Classification (NSSEC) unless stated otherwise.

Those in the lowest social class saw the greatest increase in constant stress between 2005 and 2015

The image of better paid occupations facing more stress appears to be confirmed by the first two columns of Table 4. Four in ten of those in professional or managerial occupations say that they find work stressful either "always" or "often", compared with 3 in 10 of those in semi-routine or routine occupations. However there is no linear effect of social class across all the occupational categories, and the two groups shown in Table 4 are equally likely to report that their job is *always* stressful. Moreover, those in the lowest social class saw the greatest increase in constant stress between 2005 and 2015. A similar, though less marked pattern is seen for education.

Stress at work (at least "often") is more common in the middle age groups, peaking at 43% for 35-44 year olds, while it is less frequently reported by the youngest and oldest groups (though there are small sample sizes for the youngest group). Men and women are equally likely to face stress at work (38% and 36% respectively saying this happens at least often).

Table 4 How often work is stressful, by social class, 2005 and 2015

	Social Class				All	
	Managerial & professional occupations		Semi-routine & routine occupations			
	2005	2015	2005	2015	2005	2015
	%	%	%	%	%	%
Always	8	10	1	10	7	8
Often	31	32	18	19	25	29
Unweighted base	*230*	*470*	*122*	*217*	*502*	*942*

Base: all in work

We went on to ask whether workers are prepared to 'go the extra mile' in helping their organisation to succeed:

> ***I am willing to work harder than I have to in order to help the firm or organisation I work for succeed***

Seven in ten (69%) agree they are willing to work harder than they have to

Seven in ten (69%) agree they are willing to work harder than they have to - up from 61% in 2005 and 57% in 1997. It is possible that the recession and concerns over retaining jobs could be affecting this seemingly 'altruistic' intention towards hard work, especially as most of the increase has occurred since 2005. The subgroups most likely to agree with this statement are also those most likely to be experiencing stress, which may be no coincidence. Thus it is those working in professional occupations who are the most likely to agree (77%) while the least likely are those in routine and semi-routine occupations (44%). Similarly, 75% of the 35-44 age group agree with this approach, while younger people (those aged 18-24), at 58%, are among the groups least likely to do so (though there is a small sample size for this group). Again, there is no difference by sex, or education. Perhaps this willingness to work harder than necessary is another indication of work intensification, if workplaces are now more likely to have a culture of harder work and, being present for long hours.

If the signs are that work is intensifying, might that imply that workers' conditions have worsened when it comes to questions of control and flexibility in the work environment and over the working day? These are both elements that some have linked to the intensification debate. Or do perceptions of legal rights pertaining to flexible working patterns and other working conditions mean that this area is relatively protected?

We posed three different questions on this subject, the first of which asked workers to say which of the following three statements "best describes how your working hours are decided":

> ***Starting and finishing times are decided by my employer and I cannot change them on my own***
>
> ***I can decide the time I start and finish work within certain limits***
>
> ***I am entirely free to decide when I start and finish work***

In 2015, a slight majority (54%) have no control over their working hours, with start and finish times decided by the employer. Around a third (35%) choose the second statement (meaning they have control within limits), with only 9% having complete freedom to decide their working times. There has been no improvement in workers' ability to determine their starting and finishing times - these figures are little different to findings from 2005 and 1997.

The second question asks about more occasional flexibility - how difficult it would be "to take an hour or two off during working hours, to take care of personal or family matters?" For most workers, this is something they can do without too much difficulty. Two-thirds (65%) say it would be "not too difficult" or "not difficult at all" to take an hour or two off work. However, while only a small minority - close to 1 in 6 (16%) - say it would be "very difficult" to take off an hour or two, this is up slightly from 1 in 10 (10%) in 2005.

Two-thirds (65%) say it would be "not too difficult" or "not difficult at all" to take an hour or two off work

Our third question is about the level of control workers feel they have over organising their daily work. The right-hand column in Table 5 reveals that most workers feel they have a say in this. Three in ten report being completely free to decide how to organise their daily work, while a further 4 in 10 can do so within certain limits. Taking both categories together there has been little change since 2005, but there has been an increase in the first (having complete day-to-day autonomy).

Table 5 Deciding the organisation of daily work, by social class, 2005 and 2015

	Social class				All	
	Managerial & professional occupations		Semi-routine & routine occupations			
Which best describes how your daily work is organised?	2005	2015	2005	2015	2005	2015
	%	%	%	%	%	%
I am free to decide how my daily work is organised	28	39	13	9	24	30
I can decide how my daily work is organised within certain limits	53	47	37	27	48	40
I am not free to decide how my daily work is organised	16	12	42	57	23	25
Unweighted base	*221*	*444*	*116*	*217*	*502*	*942*

Base: all in work

There are some important social class differences in whether people have freedom over how to organise their work

Again there are some important social class differences in whether people have freedom over how to organise their work (see the first four columns of Table 5), while there is a less marked relationship (but in a similar direction) with education. Only 12% of professional/managerial workers say they have no freedom to decide the organisation of their work, compared with 57% of workers in semi-routine and routine occupations. In comparing 2005 and 2012, those in semi-routine and routine occupations have experienced an increase in employer control, from 42% having no freedom to decide the organisation of daily work in 2005 to 57% in 2015. Conversely, professionals have not experienced this encroaching employer authority. They are more likely now to have freedom over organising their daily work.

So, while only a minority of workers can choose *when* to work, two-thirds have more occasional flexibility and 7 in 10 have at least some freedom about *how* they work day-to-day. Any changes over time have been small, and not all in the same direction, suggesting that these aspects of working conditions may not be related to the intensification of work that our findings on stress indicated. However, the growth in the number of better jobs may perhaps be driving the increase in stress and in autonomy for some groups.

Conclusions

Our findings suggest a fairly healthy picture in terms of public attitudes to work and experiences of work in Britain, with little sign of any lasting negative impact of the recession. Over the longer-term, we have found improvements (or stability) in many key measures relating to job satisfaction, non-financial motivations to work and perceived job quality. This isn't to say that everyone has the job attributes that they desire. For some, job security remains an elusive concept, yet it is that (along with an interesting job) that people

For some, job security remains an elusive concept, yet it is that (along with an interesting job) that people most value

most value. In many cases workers are also unable to access their desired levels of opportunity for advancement, or to have the kind of interesting job they would like.

The idea that jobs are polarising is not supported by our data. Indeed, the findings refute the view that the proportion with 'bad' jobs are growing at all, while it is clear that the percentage with 'good' jobs is rising. This is true across each of the socio-demographic subgroups we examined, with improvements (or at least stability) for workers regardless of their age, sex or social class. Even so, certain subgroups are faring worse than others. In particular, those in the lowest social class are much less likely to have a job with 4 or more positive attributes than their counterparts in the highest social class, and we have seen that this group are encountering worse terms and conditions in other areas, such as the organisation of the day-to-day content of their jobs. Older workers are another group who have poorer experiences in some areas of working life, such as having less job security than younger workers. So while there is not evidence of polarisation, there are some clues that lower status workers and older workers are not enjoying all the favourable employment terms that other groups are experiencing.

People are now facing more stress at work

Lastly, and fitting the discourses around intensification of work, people are now facing more stress at work. More are also now prepared to work beyond what is strictly necessary - a trend that may be linked to concerns about retaining their jobs in an environment where it is getting tougher to move to better or even just comparable jobs. Moreover, while many of these patterns are common to both men and women, some outcomes (such as experiencing stress) are quite strongly correlated with social class and age.

Indeed throughout much of the chapter two themes have emerged. On the one hand, the importance of social class, education and age in understanding people's working experiences, and on the other, the weaker relationship (if any) with sex. This isn't to say that there are no differences in men and women's relationship with the labour market - women still earn less than men, and significantly fewer are in paid work. But our evidence suggests that sex isn't central to these particular attitudes and experiences of work, and how they have been changing in recent years. This perhaps chimes with findings from our 29th Report chapter which found evidence that "the employment experiences of men and women have been converging in recent years" (McManus and Perry, 2012).

We end with a thought about policy implications. On the basis of our analysis, one area that remains of particular concern is that of job insecurity. There has been no perceived increase in job security between 2005 and 2015, and yet this is one of the most desired features of jobs. Some particular policy reforms relating to this (such as to zero-hours contracts) were indeed debated between the political parties during the 2015 General Election campaign, but insecurity goes much beyond that relatively small element of the labour market. This therefore represents a potential area for action for our representatives at Westminster.

References

Anderson, P. (2009), Intermediate occupations and the conceptual and empirical limitations of the hourglass economy thesis, *Work, Employment & Society*, **23(1)**: 169-180

Bryson, A., Green, F., Bridges, S. and Craig, R. (2011), 'Wellbeing, health and work', in Craig, R. and Mindell J. (eds.), *Health Survey for England – 2010: Respiratory Health*, Leeds: NHS Information Centre

Coats, D. and Lehki, R. (2008), 'Good Work': Job Quality in a Changing Economy, London: The Work Foundation

D'Arcy, C. and Gardiner, L. (2014), *Just the job – or a working compromise? The changing nature of self-employment in the UK*, London: Resolution Foundation

Donegani C. P., McKay, S. and Moro, D. (2012), 'A dimming of the 'warm glow'? Are non-profit workers in the UK still more satisfied with their jobs than other workers?' in Bryson, A. (ed.), *Advances in the Economic Analysis of Participatory and Labor-Managed Firms*, **13**: 313-32

Faccini, R. and Hackworth, C. (2010), 'Changes in output, employment and wages during recessions in the United Kingdom' in *Bank of England Quarterly Bulletin*, **1**: 43-50

Goos, M. and Manning, A. (2007), 'Lousy and lovely jobs: The rising polarization of work in Britain' in *The review of economics and statistics*, **89(1)**: 118-133

Green, F. (2006), *Demanding Work. The Paradox of Job Quality in the Affluent Economy*, Woodstock: Princeton University Press

Holmes, C. and Mayhew, K. (2012), *The changing shape of the UK job market and its implications for the bottom half of earners*, London: Resolution Foundation

Lindsay, C. (2003). A century of labour market change: 1900 to 2000. *Labour Market Trends*, **111(3)**: 133-44, available at: www.ons.gov.uk/ons/rel/lms/labour-market-trends--discontinued-/volume-111--no--3/a-century-of-labour-market-change--1900-to-2000.pdf

McKay, S. and Smith, R. (2015), The labour market before and after the recession, in Foster, L., Brunton, A., Deeming, C. and Haux, T. (eds.), *In Defence of Welfare II*, Bristol: The Policy Press

McManus, S. and Perry, J. (2012), "Work and wellbeing: Hard work? Employment, work-life balance, and wellbeing in a changing economy" in Park, A., Clery, E., Curtice, J., Phillips, M. and Utting, D. (eds.), *British Social Attitudes: the 29th Report*, London: NatCen Social Research, available at: www.natcen.ac.uk/bsa29

ONS (2016) *UK Labour Market: May 2016*, available at: www.ons.gov.uk/employmentandlabourmarket/peopleinwork/employmentandemployeetypes/bulletins/uklabourmarket/may2016

Plunkett, J. and Paulo Pessoa, J. (2013) A Polarising Crisis? The changing shape of the UK and US labour markets from 2008 to 2012, London: Resolution Foundation

Rowlingson, K. and McKay, S. (2015), *Financial Inclusion Annual Monitoring Report 2015,* University of Birmingham research report for the Friends Provident Foundation, available at: www.birmingham.ac.uk/Documents/college-social-sciences/social-policy/CHASM/annual-reports/chasm-financial-inclusion-monitoring-report-2015.pdf

Acknowledgements

NatCen Social Research is grateful to the Economic and Social Research Council (grant reference ES/L002795/1) for their financial support which enabled us to ask the questions reported in this chapter. The views expressed are those of the authors alone.

Appendix

The data on which Figure 1 is based are shown below.

Table A.1 Percentage in paid work, by age, 1984-2015

% in paid work	18-39	40-59	60+	All	*Unweighted base (18-39)*	*Unweighted base (40-59)*	*Unweighted base (60+)*	*Unweighted base (All)*
1984	65	68	11	52	*1373*	*1042*	*1040*	*3455*
1985	64	69	14	53	*820*	*548*	*431*	*1799*
1986	67	70	13	55	*1318*	*1048*	*731*	*3097*
1987	67	74	11	55	*1155*	*976*	*711*	*2842*
1989	71	74	11	56	*1213*	*1023*	*783*	*3019*
1990	69	72	12	55	*1117*	*927*	*739*	*2783*
1991	65	70	13	53	*1105*	*935*	*865*	*2905*
1993	63	65	9	50	*1172*	*904*	*855*	*2931*
1994	65	68	11	52	*1373*	*1042*	*1040*	*3455*
1995	66	66	10	52	*1428*	*1119*	*1076*	*3623*
1996	68	70	11	54	*1405*	*1121*	*1079*	*3605*
1997	63	69	9	52	*536*	*423*	*396*	*1355*
1998	70	76	9	56	*1183*	*991*	*962*	*3136*
1999	73	72	13	56	*1162*	*962*	*1017*	*3141*
2000	69	75	12	55	*1288*	*1061*	*1070*	*3419*
2001	73	73	12	57	*1199*	*1100*	*983*	*3282*
2002	72	76	11	59	*1281*	*1142*	*1008*	*3431*
2003	68	74	13	56	*1559*	*1545*	*1327*	*4431*
2004	71	77	15	59	*1099*	*1140*	*954*	*3193*
2005	71	75	13	56	*1391*	*1526*	*1349*	*4266*
2006	70	77	13	57	*1454*	*1500*	*1331*	*4285*
2007	70	77	12	57	*1362*	*1391*	*1368*	*4121*
2008	70	77	16	58	*1405*	*1563*	*1496*	*4464*
2009	70	77	17	57	*1084*	*1245*	*1087*	*3416*
2010	64	78	16	55	*1007*	*1125*	*1157*	*3289*
2011	69	75	16	56	*1030*	*1114*	*1161*	*3305*
2012	63	77	17	55	*905*	*1081*	*1256*	*3242*
2013	66	78	18	56	*952*	*1092*	*1194*	*3238*
2014	65	78	16	55	*782*	*1015*	*1073*	*2870*
2015	65	78	17	56	*1255*	*1506*	*1560*	*4321*

Base: all

The data on which Figure 2 is based are shown below.

Table A.2 Labour market trends - self-employment, trade unions and the public sector, 1984-2015 (in thousands)

Year	N in public sector	N TU members	N Self-employed
1984	+	10774	2695
1985	+	10819	2778
1986	+	10598	2789
1987	+	10480	3044
1988	+	10387	3216
1989	+	10044	3504
1990	+	9810	3542
1991	+	9489	3384
1992	+	8929	3469
1993	+	8666	3404
1994	+	8231	3516
1995	+	8031	3549
1996	+	7938	3506
1997	+	7801	3451
1998	+	7852	3346
1999	5461	7898	3305
2000	5538	7779	3254
2001	5627	7751	3294
2002	5749	7736	3338
2003	5909	7559	3568
2004	6035	7473	3624
2005	6109	7603	3644
2006	6076	7628	3749
2007	6045	7656	3822
2008	6115	7388	3846
2009	6350	7329	3870
2010	6289	7261	3990
2011	6106	7197	4057
2012	5811	7086	4224
2013	5668	7011	4262
2014	5416	6217	4558
2015	5358	6253	4574

Source: LFS (self-employed), ONS Public Sector Employment series, BIS (trade union members)

+ Consistent data not available until 1999

The data on which Figure 3 is based are shown below.

Table A.3 Perceived importance of different job attributes

Job attributes	% very important	% important
Job security	57	35
High income	13	51
Good opportunities for advancement	28	51
Interesting job	45	45
Working independently	18	46
Helping other people	21	47
Useful to society	23	45
Personal contact	20	45
Deciding own times/days of work	10	34
Unweighted base: 1793		

Base: all

The data on which Figure 4 is based are shown below.

Table A.4 Perceived importance of different job attributes, and whether workers have these in their jobs

	% say important in a job	% say have this
Job security	93	65
High income	66	26
Good opportunities for advancement	81	34
Interesting job	93	75
Working independently	68	82
Helping other people	70	79
Useful to society	70	68
Personal contact	66	91
Unweighted base: 942		

Base: all in work

The data on which Figure 5 is based are shown below.

Table A.5 Whether workers have different job attributes (score from 1-5), 1989, 1997, 2005 and 2015

Attribute	1989	1997	2005	2015
Working independently	3.88	3.92	3.9	4.09
Helping other people	3.68	3.74	3.92	4.04
Interesting job	3.88	3.7	3.77	3.9
Useful to society	3.54	3.56	3.73	3.86
Job security	3.5	3.3	3.7	3.68
Good opportunities for advancement	2.69	2.57	2.88	2.98
High income	2.6	2.45	2.6	2.77
Unweighted base	*720*	*580*	*502*	*942*

Base: all in work

NHS

Trends in dissatisfaction and attitudes to funding

This chapter explores levels of dissatisfaction with the NHS and how these have changed over time and in relation to trends in NHS funding. It examines new data identifying the reasons for NHS dissatisfaction and satisfaction. Given that the link between levels of dissatisfaction and NHS funding levels appears to be weaker than in the past, it considers how far attitudes to NHS funding may be driving dissatisfaction and if those who are dissatisfied are more supportive of particular solutions to the perceived funding problem.

Low levels of dissatisfaction

Levels of dissatisfaction with the NHS are comparatively low and remain relatively stable, despite reductions in funding since 2010.

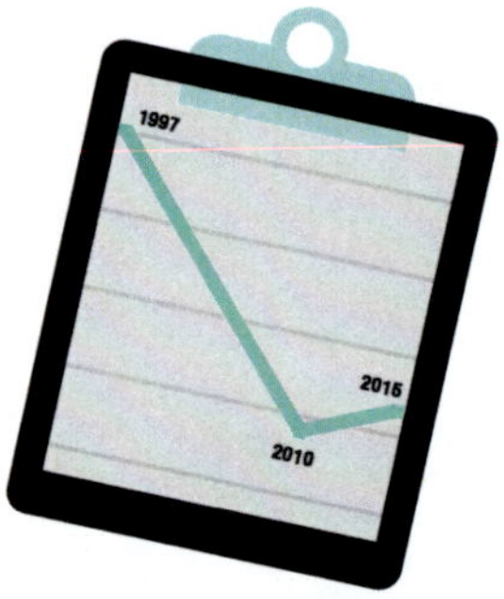

23% are dissatisfied with the NHS. This proportion declined from 50% in 1997 and levelled off between 2010 and 2015.

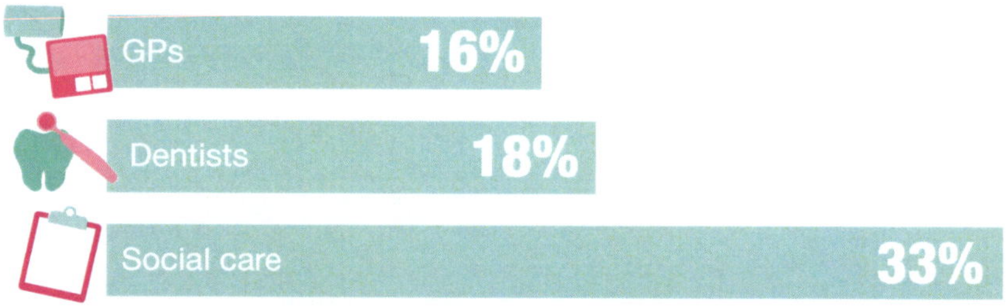

16% are dissatisfied with GPs, 18% with dentists and 33% with social care.

Dissatisfaction with NHS linked to views on NHS funding

Many of the reasons people are dissatisfied with the NHS relate to the resources it has available and those who are dissatisfied are more likely to think the NHS is facing a "severe" funding problem – yet they are no more likely to favour policy options directed at addressing this problem.

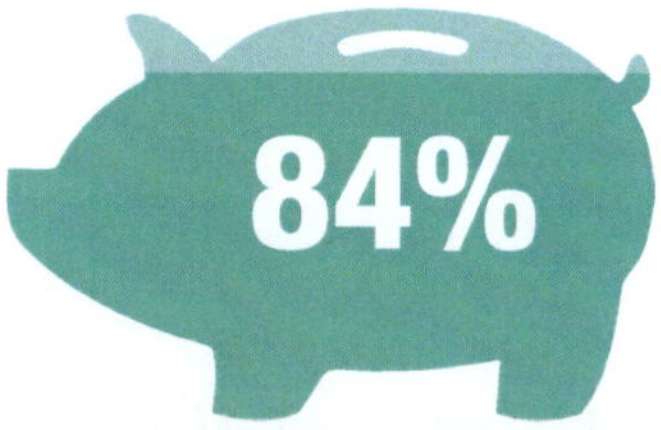

84% of those who are dissatisfied select a reason for this which relates to resources.

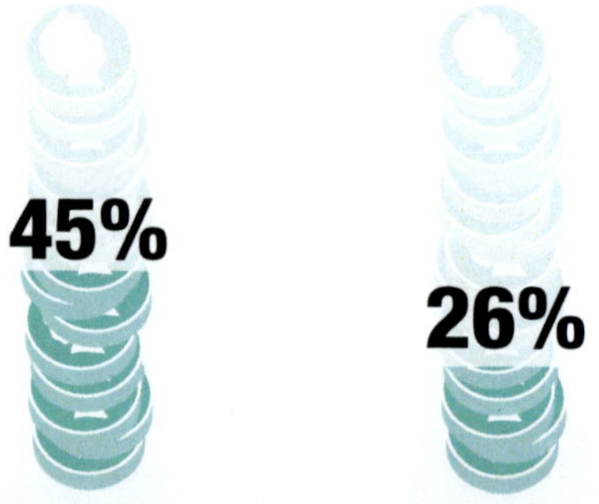

45% of those who are dissatisfied think the NHS has a "severe" funding problem compared with just 26% of those who are satisfied.

Similar proportions of those who are dissatisfied and satisfied would be willing to pay more directly for the NHS through a separate tax; however 11% of those who are dissatisfied are prepared to pay more through the current taxes they pay, compared with 19% of those who are satisfied.

Authors

John Appleby, Chief Economist, The King's Fund
Ruth Robertson, Fellow in Health Policy, The King's Fund
Eleanor Taylor, Researcher, NatCen Social Research

Levels of dissatisfaction more than halved over the 1990s and 2000s, during a period in which spending on the NHS rose

Introduction

For businesses competing in private markets, sales and profits are the bottom line. But understanding why revenues and sales change, or how profits could be improved, requires information on what customers (and potential customers) think about the quality and price of the services and products on offer. For public services, lacking (for good reasons) the basic price and profit signals of private markets, it is arguable that knowledge of what their customers think about their services is even more vital.

However, it is probably fair to say that, traditionally, the National Health Service (NHS) has not been very good at listening to the views of its patients or the public at large. But over the last decade or so it has started to invest in surveys of patients' and the public's experiences of the services they fund and use. Large-scale surveys of inpatients, users of accident and emergency services and those on GP lists for example, provide useful data to help the NHS improve its services (Care Quality Commission, 2015a; Care Quality Commission, 2015b; Ipsos MORI, 2016). The British Social Attitudes (BSA) survey provides another angle on the public's view of the NHS – and, in particular, its satisfaction with the NHS and how this is changing over time. However, just as with any private sector business, it is arguable that the data collected as part of this survey are most useful in terms of providing an indication of which sections of the population are most and least satisfied, likely causes of dissatisfaction and how this links with, and may be informed by, more general attitudes to the NHS.

While a number of BSA reports have explored satisfaction with the NHS,[1] in this chapter we focus for the first time on the sizable minority of the public, almost one-quarter (23%) in 2015, who say that they are dissatisfied. Levels of dissatisfaction more than halved over the 1990s and 2000s, during a period in which spending on the NHS rose. However, in the last five years, the downward trend has faltered but not reversed, despite one of the longest periods in NHS history of reduced spending (Nuffield Trust et al., 2015).

In this chapter, we try to understand why a sizable minority of the public is dissatisfied with the NHS and why we have witnessed the trends in dissatisfaction described above over the last two decades. To these ends, we examine how the size of the group who are dissatisfied has changed over time and if and how patterns in dissatisfaction with the NHS are reflected in relation to its component services. We consider what might be driving dissatisfaction. We explore whether there are particular sections of the public that are more likely to be dissatisfied (and whether this has changed over time) and examine new data identifying reasons for dissatisfaction (and satisfaction). Given the historic tendency for levels of dissatisfaction with the NHS rise as its funding declines, which is less evident now, in the second part of the chapter we examine the

1 For example Appleby and Robertson, 2010; Appleby et al., 2015

relationship between views on NHS funding and dissatisfaction with the NHS. In particular, we consider whether negative views of NHS funding are associated with (and may be driving) dissatisfaction and whether those who are dissatisfied are more supportive of particular solutions to addressing the perceived funding problem.

Dissatisfaction with the NHS

For more than 30 years, we have measured levels of public satisfaction with the NHS by analysing responses to the following question:

> ***All in all, how satisfied or dissatisfied would you say you are with the way in which the National Health Service runs nowadays?***

Although politicians and the media tend to focus on year-to-year changes in the public's view of the health service, by examining long-term trends we can identify broad patterns of change and the circumstances that may be encouraging or discouraging dissatisfaction.

Over the past 20 years our data paint a broadly positive picture for the NHS

As shown in Figure 1, over the past 20 years our data paint a broadly positive picture for the NHS. In 1997, satisfaction with the NHS was at the lowest point in the survey's history, with half (50%) of the public expressing dissatisfaction. Just one year later, dissatisfaction had fallen to 36% and since the turn of the century has continued to fall, down to 18% in 2010. While correlation cannot be taken for causation, it is worth noting that the period of virtually continuous decline in dissatisfaction, between 2001 and 2010, coincided with a period of unprecedented increases in NHS funding and improvement in key performance measures such as hospital waiting times (Thorlby et al., 2010).

Nevertheless, while funding growth slowed considerably from 2010 onwards, and the decline in dissatisfaction halted, there has not been a concomitant reverse, as might have been expected. Rather levels of dissatisfaction leveled off (excepting the fall in 2014), remaining relatively low by historical standards. And although dissatisfaction rose by eight percentage points, to 23%, between 2014 and 2015 this was from a very low base, as 2014 saw the lowest level of dissatisfaction with the NHS since the survey began in 1983 (15%).

Figure 1 Dissatisfaction with the NHS, 1983-2015

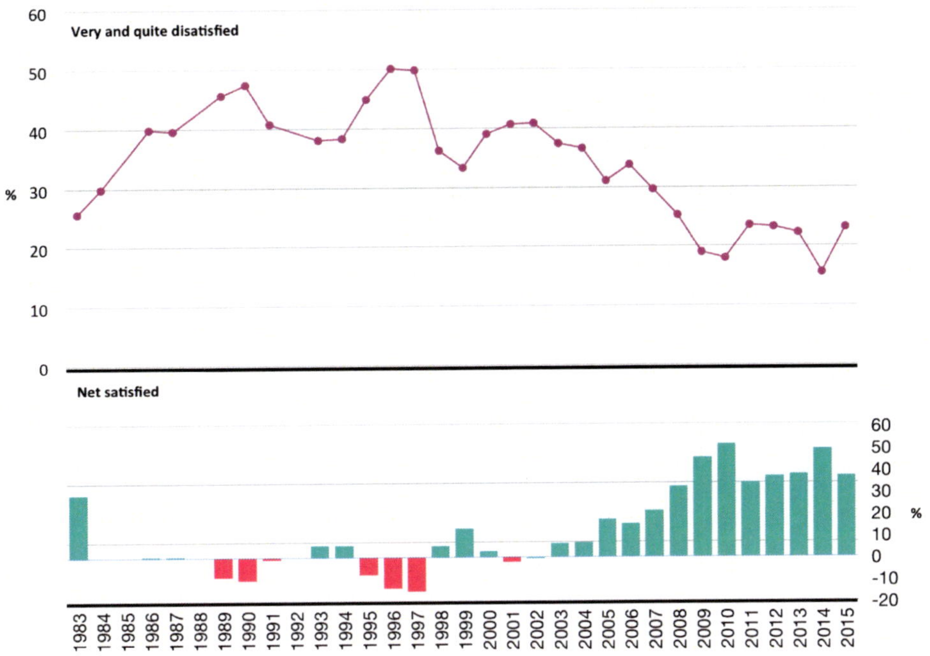

The data on which Figure 1 is based can be found in the appendix to this chapter.

General practice has traditionally been the most popular sector with dissatisfaction levels varying far less from year to year than for the NHS overall

Dissatisfaction with social care is high – 33% express dissatisfaction in 2015

Dissatisfaction with individual services

Alongside satisfaction with the NHS, we also ask respondents for their views on five individual health care services and on social care services run by local authorities. By examining dissatisfaction with these individual services, we can begin to build a picture of what might be driving dissatisfaction with the NHS overall and the extent to which this links to dissatisfaction with particular services.

As shown in Figure 2, general practice has traditionally been the most popular sector with dissatisfaction levels varying far less from year to year than for the NHS overall. In 2015, 16% were dissatisfied with GPs. Despite media attention over the past few years reporting pressures in general practice, levels of dissatisfaction in 2015 are similar to those seen a decade earlier. However, there is a small but significant upward trend over the last few years with dissatisfaction rising from 12% in 2009 to 16% in 2015.

Attitudes to dentists have seen a more dramatic change. After the turn of the century, there was a steep rise in dissatisfaction, peaking at 38% in 2004. In part, this may have been attributable to increasing problems of access to NHS dental services in some areas of the country as growing numbers of dentists developed their private work at the expense of their NHS work in reaction to changes in NHS payment rates (Department of Health, 2000). Since then, and with changes in the NHS dental contract, dissatisfaction has steadily declined, down to 18% in 2015. To find lower levels of dissatisfaction, we have to look back to the 1980s and early 1990s when, for a few years, around 10% reported negative views about dentists.

Compared with the NHS overall and its individual services, dissatisfaction with social care is high – 33% express dissatisfaction in 2015. Social care is a service provided by local authorities for people who cannot look after themselves because of illness, disability or old age. The proportion who are dissatisfied has increased from a low point of 25% in 2005, when the question was first asked albeit with slightly different wording.[2] Many people are unsure about exactly what social care services are, and relatively few people have experience of using them. This perhaps accounts for the high proportion of almost one-third (31%) who report being "neither satisfied nor dissatisfied" with the service.

Figure 2 Dissatisfaction with GPs, dentists and social care, 1983-2015

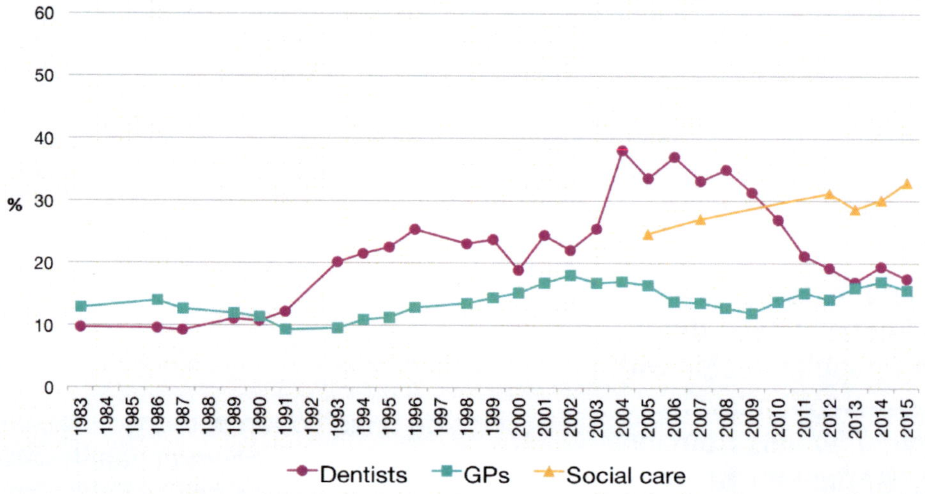

The data on which Figure 2 is based can be found in the appendix to this chapter

We also ask respondents how satisfied they are with three hospital-based services: inpatients, outpatients, and accident and emergency. Dissatisfaction levels for each of these areas has followed a broadly similar trend and tends to mirror changes in levels of dissatisfaction with the NHS overall.

While, since 2001, levels of dissatisfaction with outpatient services have been declining, down to 11% in 2015 (a slight but significant increase from the 2014 low of 8%), dissatisfaction with accident and emergency services has remained fairly flat at around 20% since 2007. On the other hand, dissatisfaction with inpatient services has tended to follow the trend for outpatients and, in 2015, recorded the second lowest level (12%) since 1983.

2 In 2005 and 2007 we asked respondents "From your own experience, or from what you have heard, please say how satisfied or dissatisfied you are with the services provided to people who need this kind of regular help with looking after themselves whose family cannot provide it?" Between 2012 and 2015 we asked respondents "And how satisfied or dissatisfied are you with social care provided by local authorities for people who cannot look after themselves because of illness, disability or old age?"

Figure 3 Dissatisfaction with outpatient, inpatient and accident and emergency services, 1983-2015

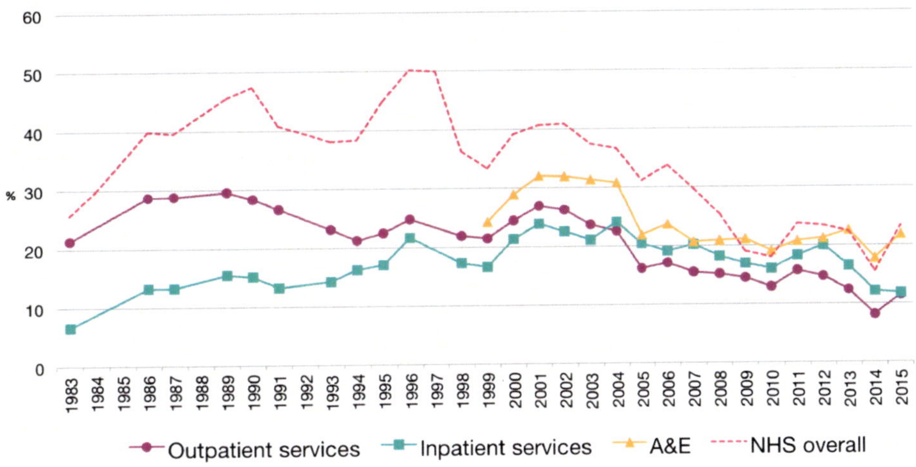

The data on which Figure 3 is based can be found in the appendix to this chapter

While we see distinct patterns in dissatisfaction with individual NHS services, dissatisfaction with hospital-based services most broadly mirrors trends in dissatisfaction with the way in which the NHS runs overall. This suggests that perceptions and experiences of these services may be important in driving levels of dissatisfaction. It is to the question of who is dissatisfied that we turn next.

Who is dissatisfied?

In this section we examine the detail underlying the broad picture of trends in NHS dissatisfaction described above. In particular, we consider whether levels of dissatisfaction are uniformly spread across the population surveyed, or whether particular groups – the young, the elderly or the better off for example – are more (or less) dissatisfied. Given the fall in dissatisfaction over the last fifteen years, how have the characteristics of the sizable minority expressing dissatisfaction changed between 2000 and 2015? Has, for example, dissatisfaction fallen more among some groups than others?

To examine this, we analysed levels of dissatisfaction with the NHS in 2000 and 2015 for groups defined by a range of socio-demographic characteristics, namely sex, age, country, ethnicity, household income and party political identification. We also examined responses by two questions, asked in the 2015 survey but not in 2000, which establish whether the individual or a family member or friend had had any contact with inpatient or outpatient services in the past year.[3] Traditionally, those who have had recent contact with a particular health service have been more likely to report higher levels of satisfaction with it (Appleby et al., 2015).

Overall, dissatisfaction dropped markedly over the 15 years between 2000 and 2015 – from 39% to 23%. Broadly, we found that this

3 Specifically, we asked respondents "In the last twelve months, have you or a close family member or close friend … been an outpatient in an NHS hospital?" and "been an inpatient in an NHS hospital?"

pattern was replicated across most of the groups we examined. Indeed, we only detected two significant differences in levels of dissatisfaction in 2000 and one in 2015. In 2000, dissatisfaction with the NHS varied significantly by age and household income, with the middle age group and the highest income quartile being the most likely to express dissatisfaction. This was the case for 44% of those aged 45-54 and 45% of those in the highest quartile of incomes in 2000, compared with a population average of 39%. In 2015, however, we did not find any significant differences by these characteristics. In fact, the only variable to emerge as significant in explaining levels of dissatisfaction with the NHS was political party identification, with the highest levels of dissatisfaction expressed by supporters of UKIP (32%) and the lowest levels by Conservative supporters (18%).

Dissatisfaction with the NHS, and the changes we have witnessed since 2000, cannot be explained to any significant degree by the changing attitudes of groups with particular socio-demographic characteristics or levels of experience of the NHS

Clearly then, dissatisfaction with the NHS, and the changes we have witnessed since 2000, cannot be explained to any significant degree by the changing attitudes of groups with particular socio-demographic characteristics or levels of experience of the NHS. It is therefore particularly timely to consider the new questions included on the 2015 survey that explore respondents' own reasons for their satisfaction or dissatisfaction with the NHS.

Why are people dissatisfied with the NHS?

To explore the factors that underlie dissatisfaction and satisfaction with the health service, we presented respondents who said that they were dissatisfied or satisfied with separate lists of nine reasons that could potentially explain their particular viewpoint. We asked them to pick up to three that applied to them.[4] The lists of reasons offered to explain dissatisfaction and satisfaction with the NHS are presented in Figures 4 and 5 respectively.

The most frequently cited reason for dissatisfaction is waiting times (selected by more than half of those who are dissatisfied)

As shown in Figure 4, the most frequently cited reason for dissatisfaction is waiting times (selected by more than half of those who are dissatisfied), followed by three factors relating to resources: that there are not enough NHS staff, that the government spends too little on the NHS, and that money is wasted in the NHS. Each of these explanations was selected by around 4 in 10. Only around a quarter of those who are dissatisfied said this was because of the quality of care provided by the service. No other reason was selected by more than one-fifth of those who are dissatisfied.

4 We included on the 2015 BSA survey design pilot the existing question measuring NHS satisfaction and followed this with an open-ended question asking respondents to explain the reasons for their response. We used the data obtained to develop a list of nine possible reasons for satisfaction and ten possible reasons for dissatisfaction that captured the range of different views expressed during the pilot and the language used by the public to describe these. The satisfaction and dissatisfaction lists were then tested on a second questionnaire pilot and refined.

Figure 4 Reasons for dissatisfaction with the NHS

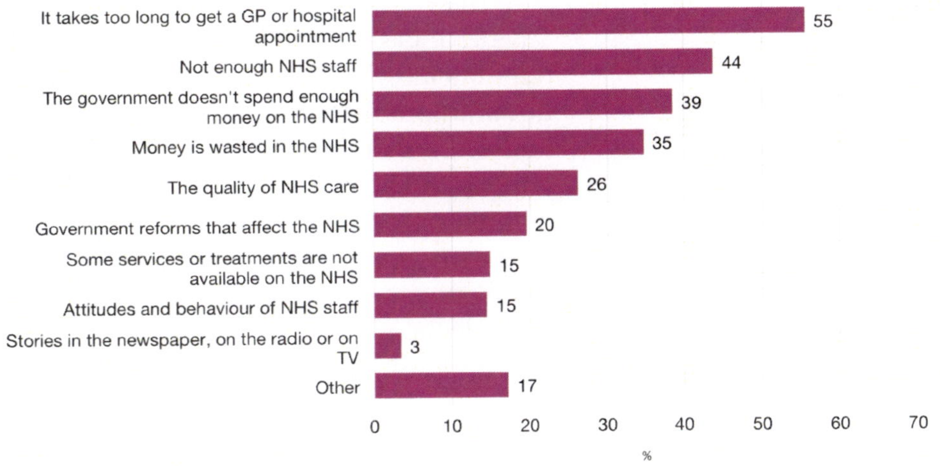

The data on which Figure 4 is based can be found in the appendix to this chapter
Base: all respondents who said they were "very" or "quite" dissatisfied with the NHS
Responses add up to more than 100% because respondents could select up to three answers that applied to them

For the 60% who are satisfied with the NHS, the quality of NHS care is the most frequently cited reason for this satisfaction

It is also helpful to examine why people are satisfied to identify where NHS organisations are doing well (and so distinguish the areas where the NHS needs to ensure standards are maintained if they want to retain public approval). Figure 5 shows that, for the 60% who are satisfied with the NHS, the quality of NHS care is the most frequently cited reason for this satisfaction (selected by 6 in 10 of those who are satisfied). This is closely followed by two factors relating to access to care: that the NHS is free at the point of use and the good range of services and treatments available on the NHS. The top five factors also include the attitudes and behavior of staff, chosen by around 4 in 10, and short waiting times for GP or hospital appointments, selected by 3 in 10.

Figure 5 Reasons for satisfaction with the NHS

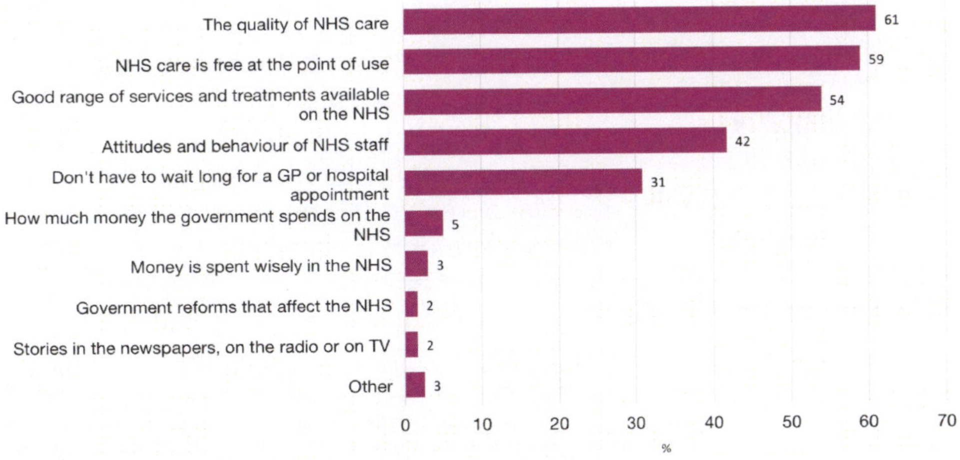

The data on which Figure 5 is based can be found in the appendix to this chapter
Base: all respondents who said they were "very" or "quite" satisfied with the NHS
Responses add up to more than 100% because respondents could select up to three answers that applied to them

Perhaps unsurprisingly, the reasons people give for being dissatisfied with the NHS are quite different from the reasons they cite for being satisfied. In Figure 6 we have illustrated this point by grouping the reasons into five broad groups:[5] resources; access to care; quality; government reforms and media stories. Categorising the data in this way shows that nearly all of those who are satisfied with the NHS cite access to care as a reason (91% of satisfied respondents selected at least one of: waiting times; care being free at the point of use; the range of services and treatments available), and more than three-quarters cite quality (76% selected the quality of care or the attitudes and behaviour of staff). Very few explain their satisfaction as relating to resources, government reforms or stories in the media. This suggests satisfaction is mainly influenced by tangible factors relating to the services people use and the ease in accessing them, rather than structural and administrative factors such as decisions made by government and NHS leaders about policy and spending.

Figure 6 Reasons for satisfaction and dissatisfaction with the NHS, grouped by theme

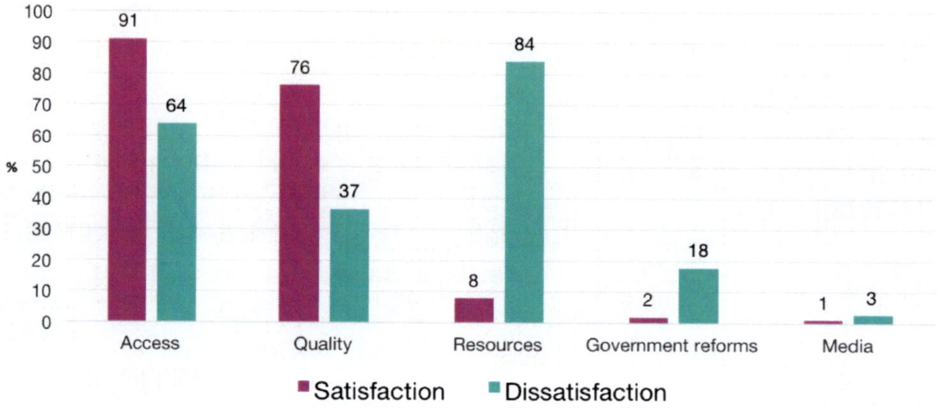

In contrast, the vast majority of people who are dissatisfied explain this on the basis of factors relating to the level of resourcing in the NHS (84% select a lack of staff, how much the government spends on the NHS or that money is wasted). A large proportion of people are also dissatisfied because of problems accessing care (this was mainly because of waiting times, but also due to the view that some services and treatments are not available). Although there has been discontent in the health service and among politicians about the major reform program that was introduced by the Health and Social Care Act in 2012, just 18% of those who are dissatisfied identify government reforms as a causal factor.

The vast majority of people who are dissatisfied explain this on the basis of factors relating to the level of resourcing in the NHS

5 **For satisfied respondents** the groupings are: access (NHS care is free at the point of use, Good range of services and treatments available on the NHS, Don't have to wait long for a GP or hospital appointment); quality (The quality of NHS care, Attitudes and behaviour of NHS staff); resources (How much money the government spends on the NHS, Money is spent wisely in the NHS); media (Stories in the newspapers, on the radio or on TV); government reforms (Government reforms that affect the NHS). **For dissatisfied respondents**: access (It takes too long to get a GP or hospital appointment, Some services or treatments are not available on the NHS); quality (The quality of NHS care, Attitudes and behaviour of NHS staff); resources (Not enough NHS staff, The government doesn't spend enough money on the NHS, Money is wasted in the NHS); media (Stories in the newspaper, on the radio or on TV); government reforms (Government reforms that affect the NHS).

How can the NHS placate these dissatisfied customers? The main message seems to be that the government should spend more money on the NHS – to increase capacity in general practice and the hospital sector in order to reduce waiting times, and to employ more staff. The results also point to the importance of the NHS being able to demonstrate that it has examined the efficiency of its operation, identified areas where money is wasted and acted on this. Meanwhile, the data on reasons for satisfaction emphasize the importance of maintaining a national health service that is free at the point of need and that provides a comprehensive range of high quality services, which can be accessed relatively quickly. These factors, which are founding principles of the NHS, seem to be closely linked to positive attitudes about the health service.

This leaves the NHS and the government with a dilemma. Growth in the NHS budget has slowed significantly since 2010 and, over the last year, many NHS organisations have started to overspend. There is little room for NHS organisations to invest in more staff or fund the extra capacity needed to reduce waiting times further. How do the public think the government should raise the extra money needed to address their main concerns? In the next section we examine attitudes to funding and how these may be driving levels of dissatisfaction with the NHS or, more positively, whether they may be suggesting funding solutions which could potentially convert dissatisfaction to satisfaction.

NHS funding

Arguably, NHS funding is a theme that cuts across many of the popular explanations for dissatisfaction with the NHS. Of the top five reasons given for dissatisfaction with the NHS (presented in Figure 4), one relates directly to NHS spending levels, three (staffing levels, waiting times and quality of care) arguably relate both directly and indirectly to funding, and one relates to the efficiency with which the NHS uses its funding (wasted money). In this section we explore the issue of funding and efficiency in more detail. We first consider whether the public feels there is a crisis in funding the NHS and if this perception may be underpinning dissatisfaction with it. Second, we examine whether those who are dissatisfied are more supportive of various policy solutions to address the perceived funding problem.

Is there an NHS funding crisis?

When we asked respondents whether they think the NHS is facing a funding problem, they overwhelmingly said yes. More than 9 in 10 (93%) support this view, with 32% identifying it as a "severe" funding problem. Moreover, although overall levels of support for this viewpoint have not changed significantly, these figures represent a shift to a more negative standpoint since 2014, when this question was first asked (where 19% identified the funding problem as "severe").

The vast majority of people who are dissatisfied explain this on the basis of factors relating to the level of resourcing in the NHS

When we consider how responses to this question vary between those who are satisfied and dissatisfied with the NHS overall, as shown in Table 1, a clear pattern emerges. Just over 1 in 10 of those who perceive that there is no problem or a "minor" funding problem are dissatisfied with the NHS, compared with 2 in 10 of those who think there is a "major" funding problem and 3 in 10 of those who think there is a "severe" funding problem. If we consider the other possible direction of the relationship between these two attitudes, we see that almost half (45%) of those who are dissatisfied think the NHS has a "severe" funding problem compared with just a quarter (26%) of those who are satisfied. Clearly then, the perception that the NHS is facing a severe funding problem links with, and may be contributing to, public dissatisfaction with it. However, it is interesting that, even for those who perceive a "severe" funding problem, levels of dissatisfaction are significantly lower than those seen for the population as a whole in 2000. This suggests that views on NHS funding are not the only factor driving levels of dissatisfaction.

Table 1 Satisfaction with the NHS, by extent to which the NHS is facing a funding problem

	View on whether the NHS has a funding problem			
	No problem, or minor funding problem	Major funding problem	Severe funding problem	All
Satisfaction with the NHS	%	%	%	%
Satisfied	72	63	47	60
Neither	15	16	21	16
Dissatisfied	13	21	31	23
Unweighted base	*179*	*510*	*346*	*2171*

What should be done about it?

Given the results presented above, one obvious policy response to reduce dissatisfaction with the NHS would seem to be to spend more money. From previous BSA surveys, we know that health is consistently the preferred choice for additional government spending. In 2015, 52% selected it as their first choice for extra government spending and 78% either as their first or second choice; the next most popular choice in both cases was education – the first choice for 25% and the first or second choice for 61%.

It is also the case that those who want higher public spending on non-health areas are less likely to be dissatisfied with the NHS than those who want higher spending on the NHS. Specifically 26% of those who select health as their first choice for extra government spending say they are dissatisfied with the NHS, compared with 22% of those who did not select health as their top priority. Furthermore, as we see in Table 2, when it comes to preferences for increasing taxes (to spend more on areas like health, education and social

Those who are dissatisfied with the NHS tend to be more in favour of increasing taxes than those who are satisfied

benefits), those who are dissatisfied with the NHS tend to be more in favour of increasing taxes than those who are satisfied – a result that makes intuitive and logical sense. Specifically, 55% of those who are dissatisfied favour increasing taxes and spending more, compared with 45% of those who are satisfied. Analysis of data from 2000 suggests that this may have historically been the case; in 2000, 55% of those who were dissatisfied favoured increasing taxes and spending more, compared with 49% of those who were satisfied. (More detailed analysis of trends in attitudes to taxation and spending is included in the chapter on Politics).

Table 2 Attitudes to government taxation and spending, by satisfaction with the NHS

	Dissatisfied	Satisfied	All	Difference (dissatisfied–satisfied)
	%	%	%	Percentage point
Reduce taxes	4	3	4	+1
Keep taxes the same	35	49	47	-14
Increase taxes	55	45	45	+10
None	5	3	3	+2
Don't know	0	1	1	-1
Unweighted base	*264*	*672*	*3266*	

Of course, it is one thing to favour raising taxes in the abstract and another to be willing to pay more personally. We asked respondents: "If the NHS needed more money, which of the following do you think you would be prepared to accept?" and provided them with the list of possible options. As Table 3 shows, 42% would be willing to pay more through taxation with around a quarter favouring some form of hypothecation for the NHS (i.e. a separate tax that is specifically earmarked for the NHS). Almost 2 in 10 would be willing to pay more via existing taxes. Among those who are dissatisfied, a similar proportion would be willing to pay more directly for the NHS through a separate tax. However, only around 1 in 10 (compared with 2 in 10 who are satisfied) are prepared to pay more through the current taxes they pay. Meanwhile 3 in 10 of the dissatisfied (compared with a quarter of the satisfied) take the harder line that the NHS needs to live within its budget.

Table 3 Acceptable options if the NHS were to need more money, by satisfaction with the NHS

	Dissatisfied	Satisfied	All	Difference (dissatisfied – satisfied)
	%	%	%	Percentage point
Pay more through separate tax - directly to NHS	24	25	24	-1
Pay more through the taxes I currently pay	11	19	17	-8
Pay £10 for each visit to a GP or local A&E department	17	16	15	+1
Pay for non-medical costs in hospital, like food and laundry	10	12	12	-2
Ending exceptions from current charges (e.g. prescription charges for children, pregnant women, retired people)	4	2	3	+2
None of the above; the NHS needs to live within its budget	30	24	26	+6
Unweighted base	*252*	*624*	*1062*	

While those who are dissatisfied with the NHS are more likely to favour increased government taxation and spending, they are no more, and sometimes less, in favour of additional specific taxation to support the NHS

Clearly then, while those who are dissatisfied with the NHS are more likely to favour increased government taxation and spending, they are no more, and sometimes less, in favour of additional specific taxation to support the NHS.

A range of alternative options to address the NHS's perceived funding problem which do not involve further government taxation are possible. One option to improve the public's view about a funding problem could be to shrink the NHS's responsibilities and activities to fit the resource it has been allocated. This could mean limiting its services to, for example, those on lower incomes, leaving others to make their own private health care arrangements through, say, private insurance. Historically we have measured public support for this option by asking our respondents whether they support or oppose the idea that, "The national health service should only be available to those on low incomes". As Table 4 shows, this has never been a particularly popular policy among the public, with around three-quarters opposing such a change between 1996, when the question was first asked, and today. Interestingly though, this option is equally unpopular among those who are satisfied or dissatisfied with the NHS (25% for both groups).

Table 4 Attitudes to limiting the NHS to those on lower incomes, 1996-2015

	1996	1997	1998	1999	2000	2001	2002	2003
NHS should only be available to those with lower incomes	%	%	%	%	%	%	%	%
Support	23	21	26	23	27	24	27	23
Oppose	75	77	72	74	71	73	72	76
Unweighted base	*3633*	*3620*	*3146*	*3426*	*2188*	*2287*	*2293*	*3199*

	2004	2006	2010	2011	2013	2014	2015
NHS should only be available to those with lower incomes	%	%	%	%	%	%	%
Support	24	24	21	26	28	32	26
Oppose	74	74	77	73	70	68	73
Unweighted base	*3193*	*2143*	*3297*	*1113*	*2189*	*917*	*1062*

So far we have seen that those who are dissatisfied with the NHS are slightly less willing to pay more for the NHS specifically through taxation and have no other discernable preference for the source of funding to fix what 45% of those who are dissatisfied see as being a "severe" funding problem. Are there other actions the NHS could take in the absence of more money being made available that the dissatisfied in particular would favour?

Table 5 presents responses to a question which asked respondents what they think the most important thing is for the NHS to do, "if demand for NHS services exceeds the amount of funding it receives". (Respondents were offered a choice of the four options presented in the table, or were able to choose "none of these"). The most popular options identified are for the NHS to stop providing treatments that are poor value for money, selected by 4 in 10, and restricting what the NHS offers by limiting access to non-emergency treatments, chosen by one in four. However, there are no significant differences in the proportions of those who are satisfied and dissatisfied with the NHS who select these, or any of the other responses.

Table 5 Views on the most important thing for the NHS to do, if demand for NHS services exceeds the amount of funding received

	All	Dissatisfied	Satisfied	Difference (dissatisfied – satisfied)
	%	%	%	Percentage point
Stop providing treatments that are poor value for money	44	42	47	-5
Restrict access to non-emergency treatment	23	26	21	+5
Raise the threshold for treatment, so people have to be sicker to receive care	9	8	9	-2
Delay treatments so people have to wait longer before they can receive treatment	2	*	3	-3
None of these	18	21	17	+3
Unweighted base	*1062*	*252*	*624*	

Maintaining low levels of dissatisfaction with the NHS cannot be achieved by policy in relation to NHS funding alone

In terms of attitudes to the funding of the NHS then, we have seen that those who are dissatisfied are distinct from those who are satisfied in terms of being more likely to think that the NHS is facing a severe funding problem – a view expressed by almost half. Yet while the dissatisfied are also more likely to support increased taxation and government spending in general, they are less likely to support an increase in the taxes they pay personally compared with those who are satisfied. They also do not express discernably different views in relation to any of the other policy options available for addressing the NHS's funding problem. This clearly suggests that maintaining low levels of dissatisfaction with the NHS cannot be achieved by policy in relation to NHS funding alone. This is a finding that is endorsed by the comparatively low levels of dissatisfaction we witness in 2015, in a period when more than 9 in 10 perceive the NHS to be experiencing a funding problem.

Conclusions

Dissatisfaction with the NHS, at 23%, remains at a relatively low level historically and appears to be in a comparatively flat period after falling fairly steadily since the turn of the century when it stood at 39%. Understanding what drives changes in dissatisfaction, not just from year to year, but over longer periods too, is important for the NHS and policy makers given their desire to improve services and the public's attitudes towards them.

There is little variation in levels of dissatisfaction by socio-demographic characteristics and, when we compare the 2015 data with that obtained in 2000, no evidence of long-term patterns in relation to this area. From a policy point of view, this suggests that a practical proposal to reduce dissatisfaction would not need to focus on one or more demographically defined group. For this reason, it is best to focus on the practical question of why some people say they are dissatisfied. On this, we find that the dissatisfied are concerned with a variety of perceived failings of the NHS, from long waiting times to the quality of care and the attitudes and behaviour of NHS staff. In particular, NHS funding and resourcing appears to relate directly or indirectly to many of the top reasons given for being dissatisfied. And indeed, while a majority of those surveyed felt the NHS was currently facing a funding problem, among the dissatisfied, slightly fewer than half felt this was severe compared with one-quarter of the satisfied.

If funding seems to be a particular problem, what would make those expressing dissatisfaction more satisfied with the NHS? One option – limiting the NHS to those on low incomes in order to fit a constrained NHS budget – was an equally minority preference among both those dissatisfied and satisfied with the NHS. While increasing taxation and government spending was more popular among the former than the latter, when asked specifically about their personal willingness to pay more for the NHS – either through a hypothecated tax or current taxes – the dissatisfied turn out to be somewhat less enthusiastic about tax increasers than the satisfied. Although more than one-third of the dissatisfied do say they would be willing to pay more through current or a new hypothecated tax, 3 in 10 take a harder line view that the NHS should live within its budget.

To talk about the dissatisfied as a uniform group is misleading. As we have seen, they have different reasons for being dissatisfied and hold different views on the solutions to funding problems

Of course, to talk about the dissatisfied as a uniform group is misleading. As we have seen, they have different reasons for being dissatisfied and hold different views on the solutions to funding problems. While for some tax and spend is the answer, for others (more concerned for example about money being wasted in the NHS) the solution is for the NHS to live within its means and reduce spending on treatments that are poor value for money. As ever, perhaps, there is no single policy action that offers a total solution.

This may not always hold however. The NHS is currently halfway through a decade of planned funding restraint. While the next five years will be as tight financially as the last five years, it starts from a very different - and more difficult - position financially and in terms of its headline performance now compared with 2010 (Nuffield Trust et al., 2015). Over nine out of ten acute hospitals in England are likely to end 2015/16 with an overspent budget for example (Appleby et al., 2016). But many are also failing on a number of key government waiting time standards. On the government's current funding plans, how the public's attitudes towards the NHS develop over the next few years - especially the connection between identifying funding as a problem and the willingness to accept solutions to that problem – may start to coalesce. Whether this will be a more favourable attitude to increased tax and spend, or a more hard-line view on the need for the NHS to live within its means or seek alternative out of pocket revenue, will depend on the ability of the NHS to not just maintain, but improve on headline performance.

References

Appleby, J., Robertson, R. (2010), 'A healthy improvement? Satisfaction with the NHS under Labour' in Park, A., Curtice, J., Clery, L., and Bryson, C. (eds.), *British Social Attitudes Survey 27th report - exploring Labour's legacy,* London: Sage

Appleby, J., Robertson, R., Taylor, E. (2015), 'Public attitudes towards the NHS in austere times' in Curtice, J. and Ormston, R. (eds.), *British Social Attitudes Survey 32nd report – the verdict on five years of coalition government*, available at: http://bsa.natcen.ac.uk/latest-report/british-social-attitudes-32/key-findings/introduction.aspx

Appleby, J., Thompson, J., and Jabbal, J. (2016), 'How is the NHS performing? Quarterly monitoring report 19', May 2016, London: The King's Fund, available at: http://qmr.kingsfund.org.uk/2016/19

Care Quality Commission (2015a), *National NHS patient survey programme. National results from the 2014 inpatient survey*. May 2015, London: The Care Quality Commission, available at: http://www.cqc.org.uk/sites/default/files/20150051 9%20NHS%20Inpatient%20Survey%202014%20National%20summary%20and%20results%20tables%20FINAL.pdf

Care Quality Commission (2015b), *Key findings from the national accident and emergency patient survey 2014*, London: The Care Quality Commission, available at: http://www.cqc.org.uk/sites/default/files/20141201_accident_and_emergency_survey_2014_key_findings.pdf

Department of Health (2000), *Modernising NHS dentistry - Implementing the NHS Plan*, London Department of Health, available at: http://webarchive.nationalarchives.gov.uk/20130107105354/http://www.dh.gov.uk/prod_consum_dh/groups/dh_digitalassets/@dh/@en/documents/digitalasset/dh_4019304.pdf

Ipsos Mori (2016), *GP patient survey – national summary report*, January 2016, London: Ipsos MORI, available at: http://gp-survey-production.s3.amazonaws.com/archive/2016/January/January+2016+National+Summary+Report.pdf

Nuffield Trust, The Health Foundation and The King's Fund (2015), *The spending review: what does it mean for health and social care?* available at: http://www.kingsfund.org.uk/sites/files/kf/field/field_publication_file/Spending-Review-Nuffield-Health-Kings-Fund-December-2015_0.pdf

Thorlby, R., Harrison, T., Foot, C., Maybin, M., Appleby, J., Ross, S. and Naylor, C. (2010), *A high performing NHS? A review of progress 1997 – 2010*, London: the King's Fund, available at: http://www.kingsfund.org.uk/publications/high-performing-nhs

Acknowledgements

NatCen Social Research would like to thank the King's Fund for funding the questions reported in this chapter. The views expressed here are those of the authors alone.

Appendix

The data for Figure 1 are as follows:

Table A.1 Satisfaction with the NHS, 1983–2015

	83	**84**	**86**	**87**	**89**	**90**	**91**	**93**	**94**	**95**
	%	%	%	%	%	%	%	%	%	%
Satisfied	55	51	40	40	37	37	40	44	44	37
Neither	20	19	19	20	18	15	19	18	17	18
Dissatisfied	26	30	40	40	46	47	41	38	38	45
Net satisfied	29	0	1	1	-9	-10	-1	6	6	-8
Unweighted base	*1761*	*1675*	*3100*	*2847*	*3029*	*2797*	*2918*	*2945*	*3469*	*3633*
	96	**97**	**98**	**99**	**00**	**01**	**02**	**03**	**04**	**05**
	%	%	%	%	%	%	%	%	%	%
Satisfied	36	34	42	46	42	39	40	44	44	48
Neither	14	15	22	20	19	20	18	18	20	20
Dissatisfied	50	50	36	33	39	41	41	37	37	31
Net satisfied	-14	-15	5	13	3	-2	-1	6	7	17
Unweighted base	*3620*	*1355*	*3146*	*3143*	*3426*	*2188*	*2287*	*2293*	*3199*	*3193*
	06	**07**	**08**	**09**	**10**	**11**	**12**	**13**	**14**	**15**
	%	%	%	%	%	%	%	%	%	%
Satisfied	49	51	58	64	70	58	61	60	65	60
Neither	16	19	16	16	12	18	16	17	19	16
Dissatisfied	34	30	25	19	18	24	23	22	15	23
Net satisfied	15	21	32	46	52	34	37	38	50	37
Unweighted base	*2143*	*3078*	*3358*	*3421*	*3297*	*1096*	*1103*	*1063*	*1937*	*2167*

The data for Figure 2 are as follows:

Table A.2 Dissatisfaction with GPs, dentists and social care, 1983–2015

	83	86	87	89	90	91	93	94	95	96
% dissatisfied	%	%	%	%	%	%	%	%	%	%
GPs	13	14	13	10	11	11	10	11	11	13
Dentists	10	10	9	20	22	23	20	22	23	25
Social care	n/a	n/a	n/a	n/a	n/a	n/a	n/a	n/a	n/a	n/a
Unweighted base	*1761*	*3100*	*2847*	*3029*	*2797*	*2918*	*2945*	*3469*	*3633*	*3620*

	98	99	00	01	02	03	04	05	06	07
% dissatisfied	%	%	%	%	%	%	%	%	%	%
GPs	14	14	15	17	18	17	17	16	14	14
Dentists	23	24	19	24	22	26	38	34	37	33
Social care	n/a	n/a	n/a	n/a	n/a	n/a	n/a	25	n/a	27
Unweighted base	*3146*	*3143*	*3426*	*2188*	*2287*	*2293*	*3199*	*3193*	*2143*	*3078*

	08	09	10	11	12	13	14	15
% dissatisfied	%	%	%	%	%	%	%	%
GPs	13	12	14	15	14	16	17	16
Dentists	35	31	27	21	19	17	19	18
Social care	n/a	n/a	n/a	n/a	31	29	30	33
Unweighted base	*3358*	*3421*	*3297*	*1096*	*1103*	*1063*	*971*	*1062*

n/a = not asked

The data for Figure 3 are as follows:

Table A.3 Dissatisfaction with outpatient services, inpatient services and A&E services, 1983–2015

	83	**86**	**87**	**89**	**90**	**91**	**93**	**94**	**95**	**96**
% dissatisfied	%	%	%	%	%	%	%	%	%	%
Outpatient services	21	29	29	30	28	27	23	21	22	25
Inpatient services	7	13	13	15	15	13	14	16	17	22
A&E	n/a	n/a	n/a	n/a	n/a	n/a	n/a	n/a	n/a	n/a
NHS overall	26	40	40	46	47	41	38	38	45	50
Unweighted base	*1761*	*3100*	*2847*	*3029*	*2797*	*2918*	*2945*	*3469*	*3633*	*3620*

	98	**99**	**00**	**01**	**02**	**03**	**04**	**05**	**06**	**07**
% dissatisfied	%	%	%	%	%	%	%	%	%	%
Outpatient services	22	21	24	27	26	24	23	16	17	16
Inpatient services	17	17	21	24	23	21	24	20	19	20
A&E	n/a	24	29	32	32	31	31	22	24	21
NHS overall	36	33	39	41	41	37	37	31	34	30
Unweighted base	*3146*	*3143*	*3426*	*2188*	*2287*	*2293*	*3199*	*3193*	*2143*	*3078*

	08	**09**	**10**	**11**	**12**	**13**	**14**	**15**
% dissatisfied	%	%	%	%	%	%	%	%
Outpatient services	15	14	13	16	15	12	8	11
Inpatient services	18	17	16	18	20	17	12	12
A&E	21	21	19	21	21	23	18	22
NHS overall	25	19	18	24	23	22	15	23
Unweighted base	*3358*	*3421*	*3297*	*1096*	*1103*	*1063*	*971*	*1062*

n/a = not asked

Politics

Political attitudes and behaviour in the wake of an intense constitutional debate

Since 2010 the UK has experienced coalition government and referendums on both electoral reform and Scottish independence. This chapter examines what effect these major constitutional developments have had on public attitudes and turnout in the 2015 general election.

Mismatch between views on coalition government and attitudes towards electoral reform

On the one hand, voters continue to be relatively sceptical of the merits of coalition government, yet are now more supportive of changing the electoral system than ever.

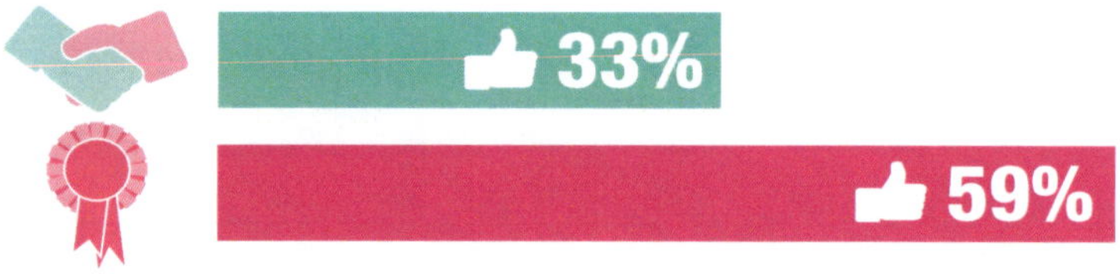

In 2010 the public mood swung strongly against having a coalition; support now stands at 33% (compared with 59% favouring single-party government).

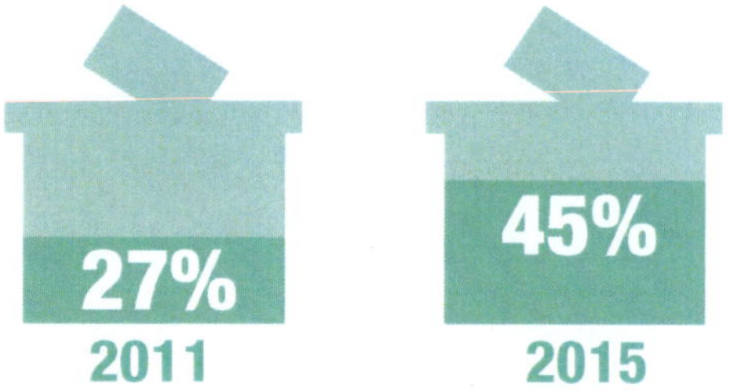

Despite this, a new record high of 45% say they are in favour of changing the electoral system (to one fairer to smaller parties), up from 27% in 2011.

No English backlash to Scottish independence debate

The independence referendum and its aftermath resulted in a higher level of support for independence in Scotland – but no sign of a backlash in England.

At 39%, support for independence in Scotland is at its highest level since 1999, up from 23% in 2012.

While in England 60% support 'English votes for English laws' this figure has not increased since the Scottish independence referendum.

Political engagement increased, but not turnout

Despite a relatively low turnout (66%) at the 2015 election, there are signs that people are somewhat more committed to the political process.

People are more likely to feel a duty to vote, to be interested in politics and to feel a strong sense of attachment to a political party. However, those without a strong sense of political commitment were particularly likely to stay at home at the 2015 general election.

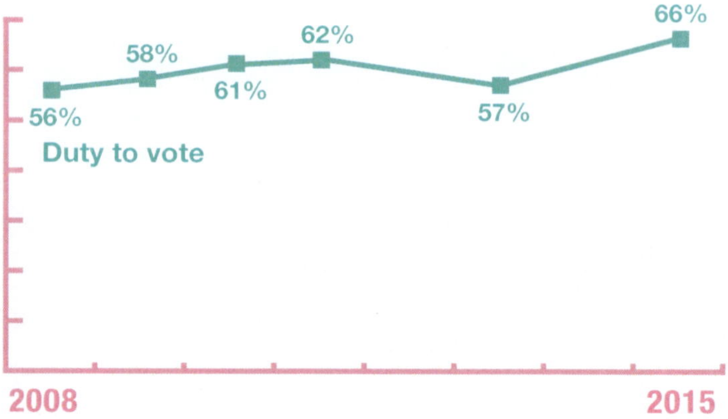

Author

John Curtice, Research Consultant, NatCen Social Research, and Professor of Politics, University of Strathclyde

Introduction

There has been considerable debate in the UK in recent years about how the country is and should be governed. First of all, between 2010 and 2015 it experienced its first peace time coalition since 1945, when, in the wake of a parliament with no overall majority, the Conservatives and the Liberal Democrats agreed to go into government together. One item in the coalition agreement between them was to hold a referendum on changing the electoral system used in elections for the House of Commons, a change that, if implemented, would likely make election outcomes that fail to give any party an overall majority more common in future (Cabinet Office, 2010). Second, the success of the Scottish National Party (SNP) in winning an overall majority in elections to the devolved Scottish Parliament in 2011 instigated a referendum on whether Scotland should become an independent country, while as soon as that was over, there was a renewed interest in proposals for changing the way England is governed. However, the counterpoint to this sometimes seemingly intense constitutional debate has been an electorate that often appears disconnected and disengaged from the political process, not least as reflected in the level of turnout in elections.

In this chapter we assess, on the one hand, how the public has reacted to these recent constitutional debates and experiences, and, on the other, the extent to which voters are engaged with the way in which they are governed. We begin by looking at the evolution of attitudes towards coalition government and the way in which the Commons is elected. We then assess people's views about how Scotland and England should be governed. Finally, we look at what does and does not appear to have motivated people to vote in the 2015 general election, and whether there is any reason to believe that the political attitudes of those who vote in elections are different from those of the population as a whole.

The experience of coalition

Responding to a question about the relative merits of single party versus coalition government is one thing when voters have only had experience of single party government, it is potentially quite another when they find themselves being ruled by a coalition for the first time. Voters might find that in practice coalition more than meets their expectations - or that it confirms their worst fears. Which proved to be the case following the formation of the Conservative-Liberal Democrat coalition in 2010 can be ascertained by looking at the pattern of responses to a question on the relative merits of single party versus coalition government:

> ***Which do you think would generally be better for Britain nowadays ....***
>
> ***...to have a government at Westminster formed by one political party on its own,***

or, to have a government at Westminster formed by two political parties together - in coalition?

Figure 1 reveals that, for much of the last 30 years or so, when the country was being run by a single party government, public opinion has been quite evenly divided on this issue. On most occasions the proportion saying they preferred a single party government was little different from the proportion stating they preferred a coalition. However, although there was no immediate reaction - in 2010, shortly after the election, the 48% who said that they preferred single party government were only a little more numerous than the 40% supported a coalition - thereafter the public mood soon swung strongly against having a coalition. The experience of a real coalition apparently served to change many a voter's mind, a change that many attribute to the Liberal Democrats' decision shortly after entering government to reverse their previous opposition to university tuition fees (Finn, 2015).

After 2010, the public mood soon swung strongly against having a coalition

Figure 1 Preference for single party or coalition government, 1983-2015

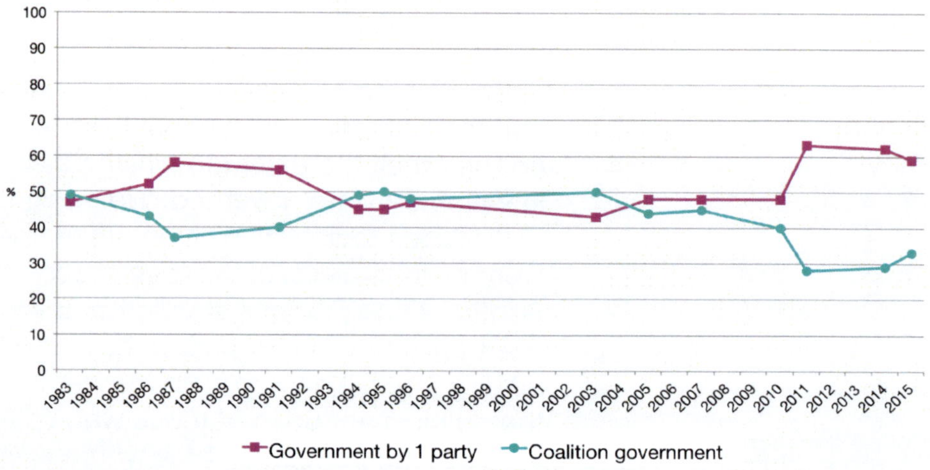

The data on which Figure 1 is based can be found in the appendix to this chapter

Meanwhile, so far at least, voters have shown little sign of swinging back again in favour of coalition government. This, perhaps, is not surprising. Now that, since the 2015 election, the Conservative party is enjoying a spell as a single party government once more, those who identify with the party are keener on that option than they were either when the coalition was in existence, or indeed when the party was in opposition. No less than 77% of Conservative supporters now say they prefer single party government, well up on the 69% who were of that view in 2011, let alone the 57% who backed that position in 2007. Meanwhile, although support for single party government among Labour supporters has fallen back from the peak of 71% that it reached in 2011, as many as 59% of them still say they prefer it to a coalition, suggesting that many of them have still not given up on the possibility that their party might be in power on its own at some point in the future.

Voters have shown little sign of swinging back again in favour of coalition government

However, a rather different picture emerges when we look at the question of changing the electoral system used in elections to the House of Commons. On this subject we have regularly asked the following question:

> ***Some people say we should change the voting system for general elections to the UK House of Commons to allow smaller political parties to get a fairer share of MPs. Others say that we should keep the voting system for the House of Commons as it is to produce effective government. Which view comes closer to your own…***
>
> ***… that we should change the voting system for the House of Commons,***
>
> ***or, keep it as it is?***

In our latest reading a new record high of 45% say they are in favour of changing the voting system

When the possibility of changing the system was actually put to voters in a referendum, held in May 2011 (albeit to a system, the Alternative Vote (AV), that is a far cry from proportional representation) it was strongly rejected. Just 32% voted in favour while 68% were opposed, although only 42% of those registered to vote actually did so (Curtice, 2013). As we can see from Figure 2, this outcome was reflected in a sharp drop of support for changing the system as registered by our regular survey question on the subject. At that point only 27%, an all-time low, backed changing the system even though just 12 months earlier a record high of 41% had said they were in favour. Now, however, following what proved to be one of the most disproportional election outcomes ever in modern British electoral history (Curtice, 2015), it appears that opinion has swung back once again. Indeed, in our latest reading a new record high of 45% say they are in favour of changing the system, almost equalling the 48% who say they would prefer to keep the system as it is.

Figure 2 Attitudes to electoral reform, 1983-2015

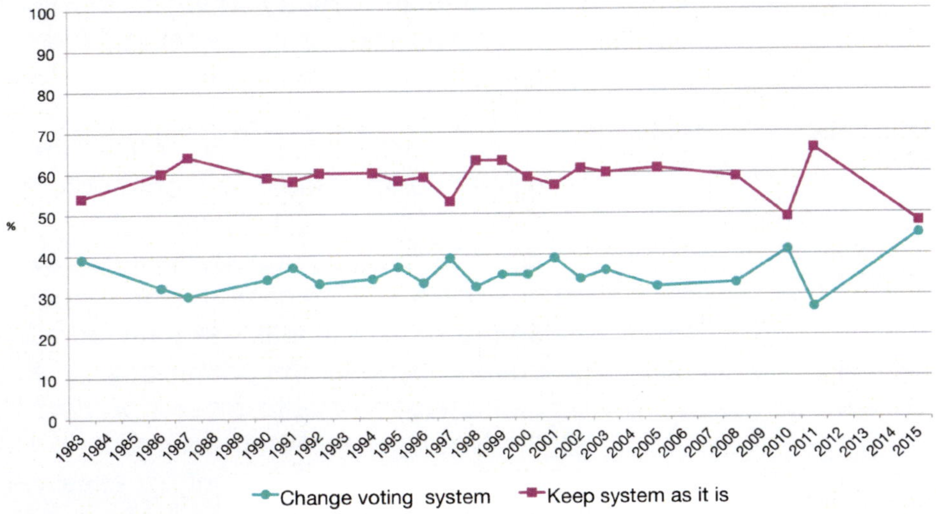

Source: 1983, 1992: British Election Study
The data on which Figure 2 is based can be found in the appendix to this chapter

On the one hand, then, voters continue to be relatively sceptical of the merits of coalition government, yet are now more supportive of changing the electoral system than ever before - even though any change along the lines described in our question on the electoral system would be likely to make coalitions more common. This would appear to suggest that many voters do not perceive the debate about the merits and consequences of electoral reform in the way that many advocates on the two sides of the argument do. Although those who would prefer single party government are less likely to back changing the electoral system than are those who like the idea of a coalition government, there are many who hold views on electoral reform that would appear to be inconsistent with their preferences for single party versus coalition government. For example, although 57% of those who prefer single party government wish to retain the current electoral system, 39% say they are in favour of change. Equally, while 59% of those who like the idea of coalition government say they are in favour of electoral reform, 38% are opposed.

The extent of the mismatch between attitudes to the kind of government that people prefer and their attitudes towards electoral reform suggests that many voters' attitudes towards electoral reform are not deeply rooted in a coherent view about the merits and consequences of different electoral systems (Curtice and Seyd, 2011). If so, that might help to explain both why it proved possible in 2011 to persuade many voters that changing the system would be disadvantageous, and why that mood has proven to be such a temporary one. Certainly, the increased unpopularity of electoral reform in 2011 was to be found both among those who preferred coalition government and those who did not, and indeed irrespective of which party a voter supported. Even among supporters of the Liberal Democrats, the party that has long been the principal advocate of electoral reform, only 46% were in favour of changing the system in 2011, while slightly more, 50%, said that they preferred to keep first past the post.

Rather than persuading voters of the merits of coalition government, the actual experience of being ruled by a coalition seems to have been to turn voters off the idea relatively rapidly, and so far there is little evidence that that mood has been reversed. However, although voters initially also swung against the idea of changing the electoral system for the House of Commons, that outlook has proven to be a more temporary one. Nevertheless, even though electoral reform now appears to be as popular as it has ever been during the last 30 years or so, it is still the case that, in response to our long-running question on the subject at least, slightly more are in favour of retaining the current first past the post system than changing to one that might be more generous to smaller parties. That, together with the fact that voters' views on the subject do not appear to be deeply rooted, suggests that it would not necessarily be easy to win support for change in any further referendum on the subject that might be held in future.

How Scotland and England should be governed

The outcome of the Scottish independence referendum, held in September 2014, not only had significant implications for Scotland's future, but also for that of the rest of the UK. After all, the UK's nuclear defence capability is located on the River Clyde, while the 'break-up' of what was once regarded as one of the most stable and important democracies in the world might have dented the UK's global reputation, standing and clout. Meanwhile, within the UK, the debate about the merits of Scottish independence was not confined to Scotland itself, but also involved the rest of the UK, not least because the SNP's plans for independence envisaged considerable continuing collaboration with the rest of the UK, including an independent Scotland using the pound as part of a monetary union.

In the event, the proposition that Scotland should become an independent country was defeated in the referendum by 45% to 55%. Nevertheless, this represented a much higher level of support for independence than might have been anticipated from survey evidence collected when the referendum was called two years previously. This is evident, for example, in the answers that people give when respondents to our sister survey, the Scottish Social Attitudes survey, are asked the following question:

> ***Which of these statements comes closest to your view?***
>
> ***Scotland should become independent, separate from the UK and the European Union***
>
> ***Scotland should become independent, separate from the UK but part of the European Union***
>
> ***Scotland should remain part of the UK, with its own elected parliament which has <u>some</u> taxation powers***
>
> ***Scotland should remain part of the UK, with its own elected parliament which has <u>no</u> taxation powers***
>
> ***Scotland should remain part of the UK <u>without</u> an elected parliament***

As can be seen from Figure 3, even after combining those who chose either of the first two responses involving independence, before the referendum never had more than 35% said that they backed independence. Indeed, the proportion had fallen to an equal all-time low of 23% just as plans for the referendum were being laid in 2012. Yet, by the time the referendum was over - and a UK general election had been held in which the SNP won half the Scottish vote and nearly all of the Scottish seats - as many as 39% were in favour. Although this proportion is still below the 45% who actually voted in favour of independence - around a quarter of respondents to the 2015 survey who said that they had voted in favour of independence

The referendum resulted in higher levels of support for independence than had been registered in Scotland since 1999

did not choose independence in response to this question - this latest reading confirms that the referendum and its aftermath resulted in higher levels of support for independence than had previously been registered in Scotland since the advent of devolution in 1999.

Figure 3 Attitudes in Scotland towards how Scotland should be governed, 1999-2015

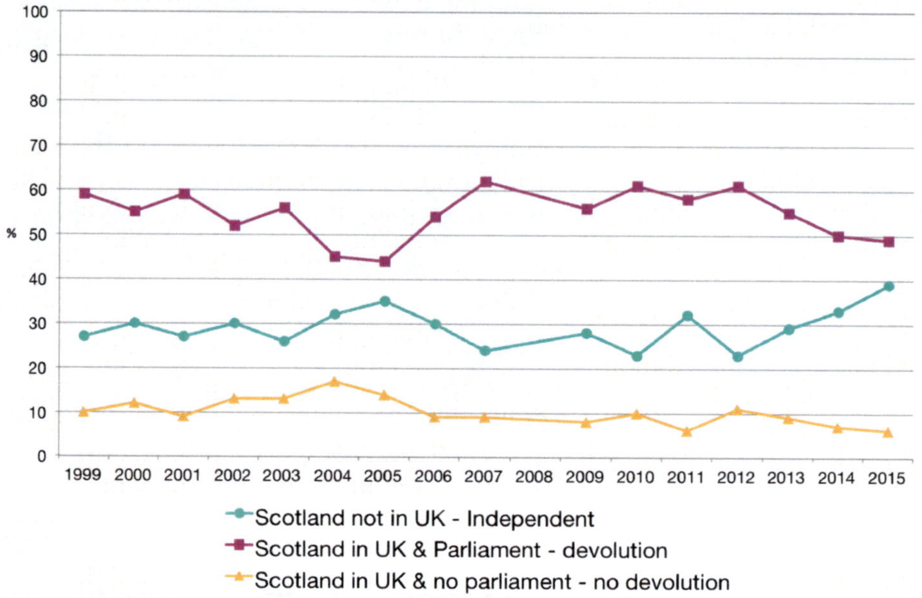

Source: Scottish Social Attitudes

The data on which Figure 3 is based can be found in the appendix to this chapter

That aftermath did not simply consist of sticking with the constitutional status quo. It was followed by the introduction of further devolution in Scotland, not least in respect of responsibility for income tax (Smith, 2015), the development of proposals for more devolution for Wales (HM Government 2015), and proposals from the Conservatives for two initiatives towards more 'devolution' in England. The first of these initiatives for England, which was already being pioneered in the Greater Manchester area, was the introduction of 'city regions' headed by directly elected Mayors. Modelled in part on the city-wide government of an elected Mayor that had been established in London in 2000, these new city regions were partly simply intended to enable local government to deliver more effectively services such as public transport, housing and economic development, that require coordination in a metropolitan area, although in Greater Manchester the new authority is now also to be vested with responsibility for NHS spending, something that has not hitherto been a local government responsibility (Sandford, 2015). The second and more immediately eye-catching proposal was the introduction of 'English votes for English laws' whereby only English MPs could vote on some stages of laws that apply exclusively to that part of the UK (Cabinet Office, 2015). For some commentators, at least, these proposals were a recognition that, stimulated by the debate about Scottish independence, people in England now also wanted greater recognition of their own interests and identity in the way in which the UK is governed (Jeffery et al., 2014).

Not that there is any immediate sign of a 'backlash' in England against the fact that Scotland enjoys a considerable and increasing measure of autonomy in its domestic affairs. In Figure 4 we show the pattern of response that has been obtained when people in England have been asked the same question about how Scotland should be governed that has also been asked regularly on the Scottish Social Attitudes survey. Although, at 19%, opposition to the idea of Scotland having its own parliament is somewhat higher now than it was when the body was first established in 1999, it still lies in the 18-23% range within which the figure has been oscillating since 2007. At the same time there is little sign that people in England are any keener now to see Scotland leave the UK than they were before the independence referendum was held.

There is little sign that people in England are any keener now to see Scotland leave the UK

Figure 4 Attitudes in England towards how Scotland should be governed, 1997-2015

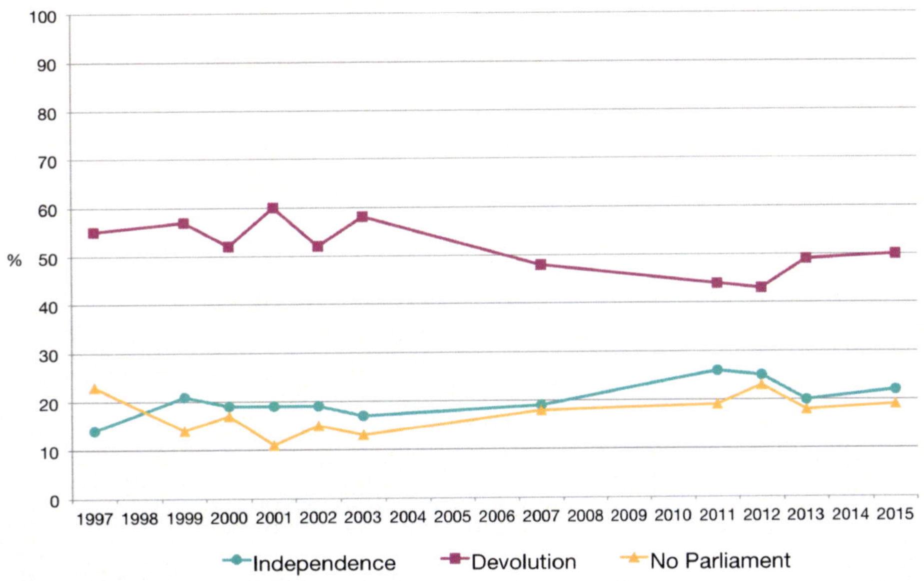

Source: 1997: British Election Study

The data on which Figure 4 is based can be found in the appendix to this chapter

Much the same impression is gained when we look at attitudes towards one of the issues that has long appeared to be a potential point of contention between voters in Scotland and those in the rest of the UK: the level of public spending north of the border. Public spending in Scotland has consistently been higher per head than in the rest of the UK and looks set to remain so for the foreseeable future, even though a significant proportion of public spending in Scotland is now due to be funded out of taxes collected north of the border (McLean et al., 2008; Bell et al., 2016). As Table 1 shows, voters in England are much more likely to say that Scotland secures more than its fair share of spending than they are to claim that it

The proportion who believe Scotland secures more than its fair share of spending is still well below half

gets less than its fair share. Even so, at 39% the proportion who believe Scotland secures more than its fair share is still well below half. Moreover, it is on a par with every other reading since 2008, since when the proportion who hold that view has consistently been between 36% and 44%. While it does appear to be the case that concern in England about Scotland's share of public spending increased at around the time the SNP first took over the reins of Scotland's devolved government in 2007, there is little sign that people in England have become increasingly critical of the position since then.

Table 1 Attitudes in England towards Scotland's share of public spending, 2000-2015

Compared with other parts of the UK, Scotland's share of government spending is...	2000	2001	2002	2003	2007	2008	2009	2010	2011	2012	2013	2015
	%	%	%	%	%	%	%	%	%	%	%	%
... much more than its fair share	8	9	9	9	16	21	18	21	22	21	18	18
... a little more than its fair share	13	15	15	13	16	20	22	17	22	23	18	21
... pretty much its fair share	42	44	44	45	38	33	30	29	30	30	37	31
... a little less than its fair share	10	8	8	8	6	3	4	3	3	4	4	7
... much less than its fair share	1	1	1	1	1	*	*	1	*	1	*	1
Don't know	25	23	22	25	22	23	25	28	23	22	22	22
Unweighted base	*1928*	*2761*	*2897*	*1917*	*859*	*982*	*980*	*913*	*967*	*937*	*925*	*940*

Base: Respondents in England only

But what of proposals for changing the governance of England, either by introducing some form of 'city-region' government or by introducing 'English votes for English laws'? Is there any indication of an increasing demand for such changes among those living in England?

Figure 5 shows how people in England have responded since the advent of devolution in the rest of the UK when presented with the following question:

> ***With all the changes going on in the way the different parts of Great Britain are run, which of the following do you think would be best for England...***
>
> ***...for England to be governed as it is now, with laws made by the UK parliament,***

for each region of England to have its own assembly that runs services like health,

or, for England as a whole to have its own new parliament with law-making powers?

The question was first crafted at a time when the principal proposal for some form of 'regional' government for England was to create assemblies in each of the 'government regions' in the country. That, for example, would have meant that both Greater Manchester and Merseyside would be part of the same 'North West' region, together with their more rural hinterland and including all of Cumbria. In the event, the idea died when, in 2004, voters in the North East region voted in a referendum against a proposal for establishing such a regional assembly there (Sandford, 2009). In contrast, the current government's proposals are for much smaller units, with each major city such as Manchester and Liverpool forming the focus of a separate 'region'. Still, if the idea of the 'city region' is a relatively popular one, we might anticipate that this would be reflected in people choosing the regional assembly option in our long-standing question.

Support for the idea of creating regional assemblies has increased

For the most part, the answers to this question over the years (see Figure 5) have suggested that there is nothing like the demand in England for some form of devolution (or more) that we have seen is evident in Scotland. Typically, rather more than half have said that England should continue to be governed as now, with its laws made by the UK parliament. However, that proportion has fallen somewhat in our most recent survey to 51%, not an unprecedentedly low figure (see the similar proportions obtained in 2003, 2008 and 2009) but certainly lower than most previous readings. At the same time, support for the idea of creating regional assemblies has increased to a level not seen since the voters of the North East turned down the idea of creating a regional assembly there. Here, perhaps, is an indication that the government's promotion of 'city regions' has helped generate a measure of popular, if far from majority, support for regional devolution within England.

Figure 5 Attitudes in England towards how England should be governed, 1999-2015

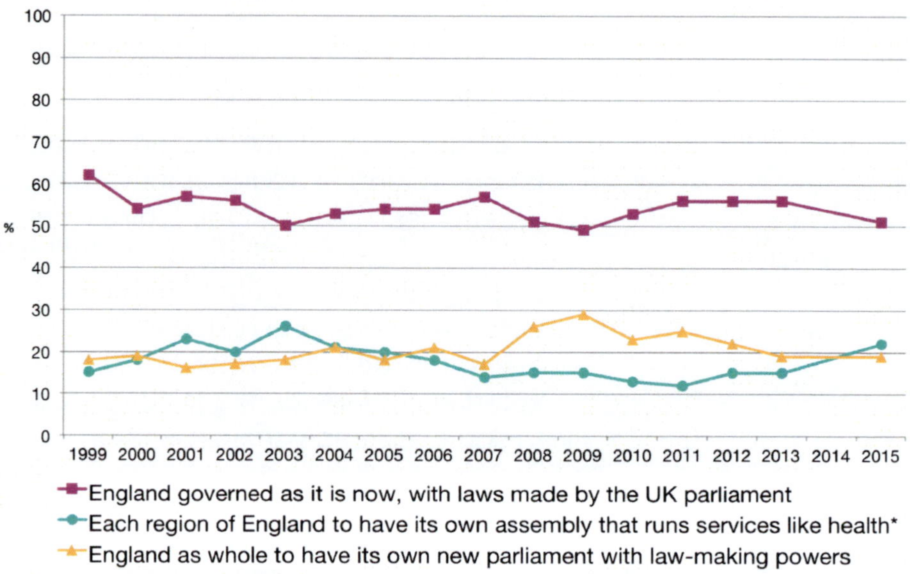

** In 2004–2006 the second option read "that makes decisions about the region's economy, planning and housing". The 2003 survey carried both versions of this option and demonstrated that the difference of wording did not make a material difference to the pattern of response. The figures quoted for 2003 are those for the two versions combined*

The data on which Figure 5 is based can be found in the appendix to this chapter.

However, if that is the case, the government has not been particularly effective at promoting the idea among its own supporters. Just 17% of those in England who identify as a Conservative supporter choose regional assemblies as their preferred option, whereas 26% of Labour supporters do so. Perhaps some Labour supporters recognise that their party is more likely than the Conservatives to win any election for a directly-elected Mayor in any 'city region'. Meanwhile, there is no sign that the idea is more popular in more urban England, where the idea has so far been most heavily, albeit not exclusively, promoted, than it is elsewhere. At 23%, support for regional assemblies among those living in the most urban parts of England is exactly the same as it is across England as a whole.

Ever since devolution a majority of people in England have agreed Scottish MPs should not be able to vote on laws that only apply in England

But if support for regional devolution, or indeed any form of devolution, in England still appears to be relatively muted, the same cannot be said of the idea of banning Scottish MPs from voting on English laws, a limited version of which was introduced into the procedures of the House of Commons shortly after the 2015 general election (Cabinet Office, 2015). As Table 2 shows, ever since the advent of devolution elsewhere in the UK, it has persistently been the case that a majority of people in England have agreed Scottish MPs should not be able to vote on laws that only apply in England. Moreover, the strength of that support, as measured by the proportion who say they "strongly" agree with the proposition, has increased from around 1 in 5 in the early years of devolution to around 3 in 10 more recently, though there is no evidence that the strength of support for 'English votes for English laws' has increased further in the immediate wake of the Scottish independence referendum.

Table 2 Attitudes in England towards banning Scottish MPs from voting on English laws, 2000-2015

	2000	2001	2003	2007	2010	2012	2013	2015
Now that Scotland has its own parliament, Scottish MPs should no longer be allowed to vote in the House of Commons on laws that only affect England	%	%	%	%	%	%	%	%
Agree strongly	18	19	22	25	31	29	30	28
Agree	45	38	38	36	35	36	34	32
Neither agree nor disagree	19	18	18	17	17	15	25	20
Disagree	8	12	10	9	6	7	7	9
Disagree strongly	1	2	1	1	1	1	1	2
Unweighted base	*1695*	*2341*	*1530*	*739*	*773*	*802*	*815*	*1576*

Base: Respondents in England only
Note: In 2013 respondents were not offered the opportunity to say 'Can't choose' (not shown in the table)

It is, however, a somewhat divisive issue politically even though, following the success of the SNP in the 2015 UK general election, Labour only has one MP from north of the border, putting it in exactly the same position as the Conservatives. As many as 77% of Conservative supporters agree with the proposition, compared with just 51% of Labour supporters. Indeed, it looks as though the political division on the subject may have sharpened somewhat - in 2013 as many as 60% of Labour supporters agreed with banning Scottish MPs from voting on Scottish laws, as did 64% in 2012. Perhaps the mood among Labour supporters has been influenced by the fact that in the event the issue is one that has been pursued by a Conservative government.

It would thus seem that, apart from some limited evidence of increased support for regional devolution in England, the reaction of people in the UK's largest country towards the debate about the UK's constitutional structure instigated by the Scottish independence referendum has proven to be a rather muted one. Being governed by Whitehall and Westminster remains the most - if far from overwhelmingly - popular option. That said, the introduction into the procedures of the House of Commons of a limited version of 'English votes for English laws' certainly reflected a long-standing mood among voters in England.

Participation in elections

One of the most notable features of the Scottish independence referendum was the very high level of turnout. No less than 85% of the registered electorate cast a ballot, more than in any previous nationwide ballot in Scotland since the advent of the mass franchise. Such a high turnout was even more remarkable given that turnouts in UK general elections have been relatively low in recent years. Indeed, in the UK general election the following May turnout (across Britain as a whole) proved once again to be on the low side. At 66%, it was only one percentage point up on the previous election in 2010, leaving it still well below what it had been at any parliamentary contest between 1922 and 1997, during which period it never fell below 71%.

Yet there are signs in our survey data that people have in fact become somewhat more committed to the political process (see also Hansard Society, 2016). One of the noticeable trends in recent years was an apparent decline in the proportion of voters who felt that they had a duty to vote when they were asked the question (Lee and Young, 2013):

> ***Which of these statements comes closest to your view about general elections? In a general election...***
>
> ***It's not really worth voting***
>
> ***People should vote only if they care who wins***
>
> ***It's everyone's duty to vote***

The proportion who say that it is "everyone's duty to vote" now stands at 66%

According to our most recent survey that decline has now been reversed. As Figure 6 shows, the proportion who say that it is "everyone's duty to vote" now stands at 66%, up by no less than 9 percentage points on when the question was last asked in 2013, and noticeably up on the 61% that was obtained immediately after the country last went to the polls in 2010.

Figure 6 Duty to vote, 1987-2015

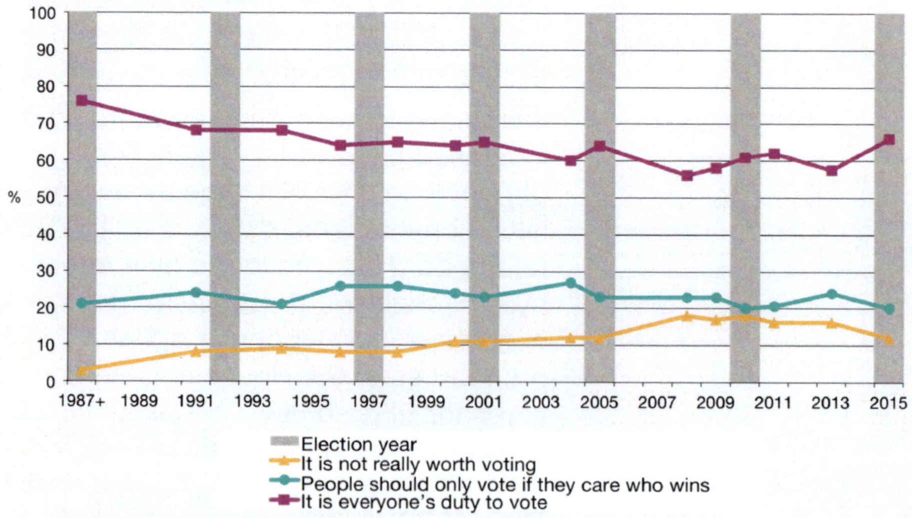

+ Source: 1987: British Election Study

The data on which Figure 6 is based can be found in the appendix to this chapter

Much the same picture is presented if we look at the extent to which people say they are interested in politics. We ask respondents:

> ***How much interest do you generally have in what is going on in politics***
>
> ***... a great deal, quite a lot, some, not very much, or, none at all?***

The proportion of the public who report "a great deal" or "quite a lot" of interest has, as Table 3 shows, tended to be remarkably stable, typically representing the outlook of around 30%. Only once, in 2008, has the figure reached as high as 35%. Yet in our most recent survey the figure stands at 36%. While not enough of an increase for us to conclude that there has necessarily been a marked stirring of interest in matters political among the public, it does make it all the more remarkable that turnout remained relatively low in the general election.

Table 3 Trend in interest in politics, selected years, 1986-2015

	1986	1991	1994	1997	1999	2001
How much interest in politics	%	%	%	%	%	%
Great deal/quite a lot	29	32	32	30	28	31
Some	31	31	35	33	34	35
Not much/none at all	39	36	33	37	38	34
Unweighted base	*1548*	*1445*	*2302*	*1355*	*3143*	*3287*

	2003	2005	2008	2010	2013	2015
How much interest in politics	%	%	%	%	%	%
Great deal/quite a lot	30	34	35	31	32	36
Some	33	34	33	34	32	33
Not much/none at all	37	32	32	34	37	32
Unweighted base	*3199*	*4268*	*1128*	*1081*	*1063*	*4328*

The proportion who feel "very" or "fairly" strongly attached to a party now stands at 41%, higher than at any election year between 1997 and 2010

One other feature of the public's attitudes towards political parties that, other things being equal, also serves to depress levels of participation is the proportion who do not feel any sense of attachment to a political party.[1] As Table 4 shows, that proportion doubled between 1987 and 2010 from 8% to 16%. Conversely, the proportion who feel either "very" or "'fairly" strongly attached to one of the parties fell over the same period from 46% to 36%. However, it appears that this change too has been somewhat reversed. True, at 15%, the proportion who do not feel attached to any political party is much the same as it was five years ago, but the proportion who feel "very" or "fairly" strongly attached to a party now stands at 41%, higher than at any election year between 1997 and 2010.

1 See the Technical Details for full details of the questions asked about people's party identification.

Table 4 Trends in strength of party identification, election years between 1987 and 2015

	1987	1997	2001	2005	2010	2015
Strength of party identification	%	%	%	%	%	%
Very strong	11	10	7	7	7	9
Fairly strong	35	27	29	28	29	32
Not very strong	40	46	49	46	41	38
None	8	10	12	13	16	15
Unweighted base	*2847*	*1355*	*3282*	*4268*	*3297*	*4328*

It would thus seem that voters were, if anything, more strongly motivated to go to the polls in 2015 than they had been at other recent general elections. They were more likely to feel a duty to vote, were a little more likely to be interested in politics, and were more likely to feel a strong sense of attachment to the political party. Perhaps, then, the explanation for the failure of turnout to increase very much lies in voters' perceptions of what was at stake. Maybe they felt that it would not make much difference who won the election; after all, the Conservatives had demonstrated a willingness to share power with the Liberal Democrats, while Labour accepted the need for further reductions in the country's fiscal deficit. If so, this perception might have reduced voters' impetus to go to the polls.

Table 5 shows the extent to which voters thought there was a difference between the Conservative and Labour parties in 2015, and how this compares with their perceptions at each and every election since 1964. We asked respondents:

> ***Now considering everything the Conservative and Labour parties stand for, would you say that that ...***
>
> ***... there is a great difference between them,***
>
> ***some difference,***
>
> ***or, not much difference?***

As we can see, voters were, if anything, slightly more likely to think there is a "great difference" now between the parties than they were in 2010. They were certainly much more likely to be of that view than they were in 2001 and 2005, when the experience of a relatively centrist 'New Labour' government appears to have persuaded voters that there was less of a difference between the parties than for at least the last 30 years. True, at 27%, the most recent proportion is still below that recorded at any time before 2001, and thus voters are still less likely to feel that there is a great deal at stake in a general election than they once did. But even so, there is nothing in these figures to suggest that voters' apparent increased commitment to the political process was negated by an increased feeling that there was little to separate the parties.

Table 5 Perceived difference between the parties, 1964-2015

	1964	1966	1970	Feb-74	Oct-74	1979	1983
	%	%	%	%	%	%	%
Great difference	48	44	33	34	40	48	88
Some	25	27	28	30	30	30	10
Not much	27	29	39	36	30	22	7
Unweighted base	*1699*	*1804*	*1780*	*2391*	*2332*	*1826*	*3893*

	1987	1992	1997	2001	2005	2010	2015
	%	%	%	%	%	%	%
Great difference	85	56	33	17	13	23	27
Some	11	32	43	39	43	43	42
Not much	5	12	24	44	44	34	31
Unweighted base	*3776*	*1794*	*2836*	*1076*	*1049*	*1035*	*2056*

Source: 1964-1997: British Election Study.[2] Figures for 1964-1992 as quoted in Crewe et al. (1995)
Respondents saying "don't know" or who refused to answer have been excluded

Among those with "not much" or no interest in politics at all, the proportion who claim to have voted was as low as 45%

The explanation for the failure of turnout to increase appears to lie in the fact that while those voters with a strong sense of political commitment were indeed just as likely to make it to the polls as before, those without that sense of commitment were particularly likely to stay at home. This pattern is apparent, for example, if we look at the reported level of turnout at recent elections according to how interested people say they are in politics (see Table 6). Whereas no less than 87% of those who say they have a "great deal" or "quite a lot" of interest in politics claim to have voted, among those with "not much" or no interest in politics at all, the proportion was as low as 45%, lower than at any other recent general election.

Table 6 Political interest and electoral participation, 1997-2015

% who voted	1997	2001	2005	2010	2015
Interest in politics					
Great deal/quite a lot	87	81	82	86	87
Some	81	72	72	71	77
Not much/None at all	67	51	52	53	45

Source: 1997: British Election Study
The bases for Table 6 can be found in the appendix to this chapter

A not dissimilar pattern is in evidence if we undertake an equivalent analysis of turnout by whether or not people feel a sense of duty to vote. As can be seen in Table 7, no less than 84% of those who feel that there is a duty to vote report having cast a ballot in the 2015

2 Between 1964 and October 1974 the question read, 'Considering everything the parties stand for would you say there is a good deal of difference between them, some difference or not much difference?'.

Just 24% of those who say that "it's not really worth voting" claim to have voted

election. In contrast just 24% of those who say that "it's not really worth voting" claim to have voted, a proportion which is lower (albeit not significantly so) than the 31% who did so in 2010, although it is no lower than the equivalent proportion in 2001 and 2005.

Table 7 Turnout, by civic duty, 1987-2015

% who voted	1987	2001	2005	2010	2015
It's not really worth voting	37	24	24	31	24
People should only vote if they care who wins	75	49	50	60	54
It's everyone's duty to vote	92	85	85	86	84

Source: 1987: British Election Study

The bases for Table 7 can be found in the appendix to this chapter

Quite why voters who were not strongly motivated to vote were particularly disinclined to vote at this election is not immediately apparent. One possibility is that the focus during much of the campaign on 'process' questions about which party might be willing to do a deal with whom in the event that no single party were to win an overall majority (as anticipated by the opinion polls), did not capture the imagination of those with little interest in politics (Cowley and Kavanagh, 2016). Certainly those with little or no interest in politics (17%) are much more likely than those with "a great deal" or "quite a lot" of interest in politics (3%) to say they do not know whether they prefer single party or coalition government, a pattern that is not necessarily in evidence on other questions in our survey.

Low levels of turnout are often a source of considerable concern. One reason is that if turnout is relatively low, there is seemingly a greater risk that those who make it to the polling station are not representative of the public as a whole (Citrin et al., 2003). In that event the outcome of an election may not necessarily reflect the views of the majority of voters. Certainly those who belong to some social groups are more likely to vote than others. A particularly striking example is the difference between the level of participation among younger and that among older people. As Table 8 shows, such a difference has always been in evidence, but when turnout first fell markedly in 2001, it did so particularly among those aged less than 45, and this pattern was repeated in 2005 and 2010 (although the figure for 18-24 year olds in 2010 should be treated with caution as it comprised fewer than 100 respondents). Unsurprisingly therefore, the age gap in turnout was in evidence once again at the most recent election, although it is not quite as big as it was at the three previous elections.

The age gap in turnout was in evidence once again at the most recent election

Table 8 Turnout by age, 1997-2015

% voted in	18-24	25-34	35-44	45-54	55-64	65+
1997	61	68	78	85	89	87
2001	43	55	65	78	74	82
2005	40	55	66	76	80	85
2010	45	49	67	75	84	88
2015	56	55	64	75	80	84

The bases for Table 8 can be found in the appendix to this chapter

Although the difference in turnout by age is the biggest, it is not the only one of note. In particular, those who are engaged in routine or semi-routine occupations (60%) are also less likely to vote than those in a professional and managerial job (80%). All in all, there would thus appear to be plenty of scope for the attitudes of those who participate in elections to be different from those who do not.

First, let us address this question by looking at the issue that is arguably central to most elections, and is certainly one whose salience has been particularly marked since the financial crash of 2008, namely what the level of public spending and taxation should be. Ever since the first British Social Attitudes survey in 1983 we have asked:

> ***Suppose the government had to choose between the three options on this card. Which do you think it should choose?***
>
> ***Reduce taxes and spend less on health, education and social benefits***
>
> ***Keep taxes and spending on these services at the same level as now***
>
> ***Increase taxes and spend more on health, education and social benefits***

As Figure 7 shows, the distribution of responses to this question has changed quite considerably over time. The proportion who said that taxation and spending should be increased rose during the 1980s and 1990s, and was still as high as 63% in 2002. But thereafter the then Labour government presided over a substantial increase in public spending and the proportion began to fall away. By 2010, shortly after the financial crash did serious damage to the health of the government's finances, only 32% wanted more taxation and spending. On coming to power that year, the Coalition government formed by the Conservatives and the Liberal Democrats, embarked on a programme of public expenditure cuts in an attempt to reduce the fiscal deficit, a decision to which the public might have been expected to react by swinging back again in favour of more spending (Curtice, 2010). However, until now there was little sign of any such reaction. Even four years into the programme of expenditure cuts, still only 37% said that they would like taxation and spending to increase.

Figure 7 Attitudes to taxation and spending on health, education and social benefits, 1983–2015

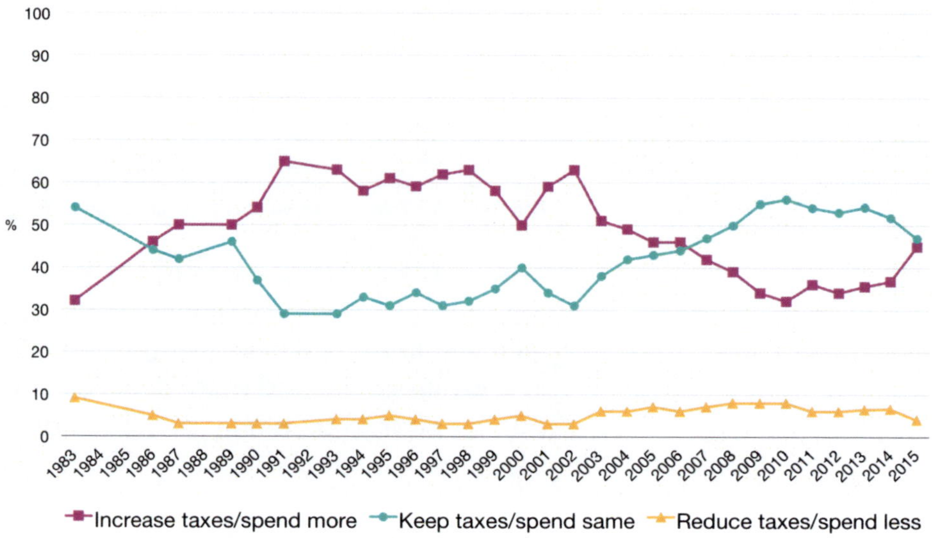

The data on which Figure 7 is based can be found in the appendix to this chapter

45% now say that taxes and spending should be increased, the highest proportion for nearly 10 years

However, there are now signs that this mood may finally be changing. In our latest survey as many as 45% now say that taxes and spending should be increased, the highest proportion to have done so for nearly 10 years. It is, though, a change that might be thought to be at odds with the fact that the Conservatives managed to win an overall majority in the 2015 election. Perhaps the explanation lies in the fact that those who were in favour of more spending and taxation were less likely to go to the polls, thereby delivering the Conservatives a majority they might not otherwise have obtained?

Of this, however, there is little sign. In fact, if anything, those who are in favour of increased taxation and spending (76%) were more likely to vote in the 2015 election than were those who felt that the level of taxation and spending should remain as it is (67%) or the (relatively small) group of people who would like a reduction (64%). As a result, among those who voted in the 2015 election, slightly more people were in favour of increased spending and taxation (49%) than wanted to keep taxation and spending as they are (45%). Still, while these differences may not help us account for the Conservatives' electoral success, they would seem to suggest that the views of those who participated in the 2015 election are not necessarily representative of the public as a whole.

For the most part, the views of those who turned out to vote in 2015 prove to be quite similar to those of the country as a whole

However, this finding is not typical. For the most part, the views of those who turned out to vote in 2015 prove to be quite similar to those of the country as a whole. This is even true of other questions in our survey that address various aspects of public spending and the delivery of public services. For example, at 24%, the proportion of those who voted in the 2015 election who agree that "benefits for unemployed people are too low and cause hardship" is exactly the same as that for respondents to the survey as a whole. The same is true of the 59% who believe that "benefits for unemployed people are too high and discourage them from finding jobs". Meanwhile, among those who voted in the election, 25% support limiting the NHS to those on lower incomes, while 55% are opposed, very similar to the equivalent figures for all respondents of 26% and 54% respectively.

Much the same pattern is also to be found if, instead of looking at attitudes towards specific aspects of public spending, we also look at people's underlying views on the issue that lies at the heart of the division between those on the left and those on the right in British politics, that is the extent to which the government should intervene in the economy with a view to securing greater equality. This underlying attitudinal dimension is addressed by the set of questions that compromise our left-right scale, details of which are to be found in the technical appendix. The scale runs from 1 (left) to 5 (right). Among those who turned out in the 2015 election, 56% had a score of 2.5 or less, thereby classifying them as being inclined towards the left. At 58%, the equivalent figure for all respondents is only a little higher.

Conclusions

In some respects, the UK's intense constitutional debate and experience in recent years has left its mark. We are, for the time being at least, none too enamoured of being governed by a coalition. More people in Scotland now support independence for their country, albeit they still constitute a minority of voters north of the border. Meanwhile in England a measure of interest in the idea of regional devolution seems to have emerged for the first time since the idea was knocked back by the voters of the North East of England.

In other respects it is remarkable how little impression the debate seems to have made on public opinion

Yet in other respects it is remarkable how little impression the debate seems to have made on public opinion. The sharp swing against the idea of changing the electoral system used in elections to the House of Commons that was in evidence on the occasion of the referendum on the Alternative Vote in 2011 has disappeared entirely, though this does not necessarily mean that the idea is now a particularly popular one. People in England have not reacted to the Scottish independence debate by adopting a more critical outlook towards Scotland's place in the Union than they did already, though the introduction of at least a limited form of 'English votes for English laws' is an acknowledgement of a long-standing grievance among voters in England.

At first glance, then, it is not surprising that these major constitutional debates did not ensure that significantly more voters made it to the polls in the 2015 general election. Voters were for the most part apparently not moved by the arguments. Nevertheless, there are signs that some of the decline in political commitment among the electorate has been reversed, including not least an increase in the proportion who believe that they do have a duty to vote at election time. Yet for those who lack commitment to or interest in politics, an election in which much of the campaign was dominated by arguments about process seems to have done little to encourage them to participate, albeit that the views of those who did vote seem to have been reasonably representative of the electorate as a whole.

As a result, for all its intensity, it is far from clear that the recent constitutional debate has done much to resolve any of the key questions about how Britain is and should be governed. The question of whether or not Scotland should remain part of the UK now divides voters north of the border. Attitudes towards the electoral system used in Commons elections appear to rest on weak foundations. While voters in England are not sure about devolution, only half of them endorse the status quo of rule from Westminster, and they might yet come to the conclusion that the version of 'English votes for English laws' that has now been put in place is inadequate. Meanwhile, getting voters to make it to the polls at all is still proving to be difficult. The days when Britain was a country that was confident in the stability and strength of its democracy still seem a long way away.

References

Bell, D., Eiser, D. and Phillips, D. (2016), *Scotland's Fiscal Framework: Assessing the Agreement*, London: Institute for Fiscal Studies, available at: www.ifs.org.uk/uploads/publications/wps/wp201605.pdf

Cabinet Office (2010), *The Coalition: our programme for government*, London: Cabinet Office

Cabinet Office (2015), *English Votes for English Laws: An Explanatory Guide to the Proposals,* London: Cabinet Office

Citrin, J, Schickler, E. and Sides, J. (2003), 'What if everyone voted? Simulating the impact of increased turnout in Senate elections', *American Journal of Political Science*, **47(1)**: 75-90

Crewe, I., Fox, A., and Day, N. (1995), *The British Electorate, 1963-1992*, Cambridge: Cambridge University Press

Cowley, P. and Kavanagh, D. (2016), *The British General Election of 2015,* Basingstoke: Palgrave Macmillan

Curtice, J. (2010), 'Thermostat or Weather Vane? How the public has reacted to New Labour Government', in Park, A., Curtice, J., Thomson, K., Phillips, M. and Clery, E. (eds.), *British Social Attitudes: the 26th report*, London: Sage

Curtice, J. (2013), 'Politicians, Voters and Democracy: the 2011 referendum on the Alternative Vote, *Electoral Studies*, **32(2)**: 215-23

Curtice, J. (2015), 'A Return to Normality? How the electoral system operated', *Parliamentary Affairs*, **68(1)**: 25-40

Curtice, J. and Seyd, B. (2011), 'Attitudes to voting rules and electoral system preferences: evidence from the 1999 and 2003 Scottish Parliament elections', *Electoral Studies* **30(1)**: 184-200

Finn, M. (2015), 'The Coalition and the Liberal Democrats', in A. Seldon and M. Finn (eds.), *The Coalition Effect 2010-2015*, Cambridge University Press

Hansard Society (2016), *Audit of Political Engagement 13: The 2016 Report*, London: Hansard Society for Parliamentary Government, available at: www.auditofpoliticalengagement.org/assets/media/reports/Audit-of-Political-Engagement-13-2016.pdf

HM Government (2015), *Powers for a Purpose: Towards a Lasting Devolution Settlement for Wales*, Cm 9020, London: Her Majesty's Stationery Office

Jeffery, C., Wyn Jones, R., Henderson, A., Scully, R. and Lodge, C. (2014), *Taking England Seriously: The New English Politics*, available at: www.centreonconstitutionalchange.ac.uk/sites/default/files/news/Taking%20England%20Seriously_The%20New%20English%20Politics.pdf

Lee, L. and Young, P. (2013), 'Disengaged Britain? Political interest and participation over 30 years', in Park, A., Bryson, C., Clery, E., Curtice, J. and Phillips, M. (eds.), *British Social Attitudes: the 30th*

Report, London: NatCen Social Research, available at: www.bsa.natcen.ac.uk

McLean, I., Schmuecker, K. and Lodge, G. (2008), *Fair Shares? Barnett and the politics of public expenditure*, London: IPPR, available at: www.ippr.org/publications/fair-shares-barnett-and-the-politics-of-public-expenditure

Sandford, M. (ed.) (2009), *The Northern Veto*, Manchester: Manchester University Press

Sandford, M. (2015), *Cities and Local Government Devolution Bill 2015-16.* House of Commons Library Briefing Paper CBP07322, London: House of Commons Library

Smith, Lord (chmn.) (2015), *Report of the Smith Commission for further devolution of powers for the Scottish Parliament*, available at: www.smith-commission.scot

Appendix

Tables

The data on which Figure 1 is based are as follows:

Table A.1 Preference for single party or coalition government, 1983-2015

	1983	1986	1987	1991	1994	1995	1996
Government by 1 party	47	52	58	56	45	45	47
Coalition	49	43	37	40	49	50	48
Don't know	4	4	3	3	6	4	5
Unweighted base	*1761*	*1548*	*1410*	*1445*	*1137*	*1227*	*1180*

	2003	2005	2007	2010	2011	2014	2015
Government by 1 party	43	48	48	48	63	62	59
Coalition	50	44	45	40	28	29	33
Don't know	6	8	7	11	9	8	8
Unweighted base	*1160*	*1075*	*992*	*1081*	*2215*	*971*	*2140*

The data on which Figure 2 is based are as follows:

Table A.2 Attitudes to electoral reform, 1986-2015

	1983	1986	1987	1990	1991	1992	1994	1995	1996	1997	1998
	%	%	%	%	%	%	%	%	%	%	%
Change voting system	39	32	30	34	37	33	34	37	33	39	32
Keep system as it is	54	60	64	59	58	60	60	58	59	53	63
Unweighted base	*3955*	*1548*	*1410*	*1397*	*1445*	*3534*	*1137*	*1227*	*1196*	*1355*	*1035*

	1999	2000	2001	2002	2003	2005	2008	2010	2011	2015
	%	%	%	%	%	%	%	%	%	%
Change voting system	35	35	39	34	36	32	33	41	27	45
Keep system as it is	63	59	57	61	60	61	59	49	66	48
Unweighted base	*1060*	*2293*	*1099*	*2287*	*1160*	*1075*	*1128*	*1081*	*2215*	*2140*

Source: 1983, 1992: British Election Study

The data on which Figure 3 is based are as follows:

Table A.3 Attitudes <u>in Scotland</u> towards how Scotland should be governed, 1999-2015

	1999	2000	2001	2002	2003	2004	2005	2006
	%	%	%	%	%	%	%	%
Scotland not in UK - **Independent**	27	30	27	30	26	32	35	30
Scotland in UK & parliament - **Devolution**	59	55	59	52	56	45	44	54
Scotland in UK & no parliament – **No devolution**	10	12	9	13	13	17	14	9
Don't know / Not answered	5	3	4	6	6	5	8	7
Unweighted base	*1482*	*1663*	*1605*	*1665*	*1508*	*1637*	*1549*	*1594*

	2007	2009	2010	2011	2012	2013	2014	2015
	%	%	%	%	%	%	%	%
Scotland not in UK - **Independent**	24	28	23	32	23	29	33	39
Scotland in UK & parliament - **Devolution**	62	56	61	58	61	55	50	49
Scotland in UK & no parliament – **No devolution**	9	8	10	6	11	9	7	6
Don't know / Not answered	5	8	5	5	5	8	10	6
Unweighted base	*1508*	*1482*	*1495*	*1197*	*1229*	*1497*	*1501*	*1288*

Source: Scottish Social Attitudes

The data on which Figure 4 is based are as follows:

Table A.4 Attitudes in England towards how Scotland should be governed, 1997-2015

	1997	1999	2000	2001	2002	2003	2007	2011	2012	2013	2015
	%	%	%	%	%	%	%	%	%	%	%
Independence	14	21	19	19	19	17	19	26	25	20	22
Devolution	55	57	52	60	52	58	48	44	43	49	50
No parliament	23	14	17	11	15	13	18	19	23	18	19
Unweighted base	*2536*	*902*	*1928*	*2761*	*1924*	*1917*	*859*	*967*	*939*	*925*	*1865*

Source: 1997: British Election Study

Base: Respondents in England only

The data on which Figure 5 is based are as follows:

Table A.5 Attitudes in England towards how England should be governed, 1999-2015

	1999	2000	2001	2002	2003	2004	2005	2006
Following is best for England...	%	%	%	%	%	%	%	%
England governed as it is now, with laws made by the UK parliament	62	54	57	56	50	53	54	54
Each region of England to have its own assembly that runs services like health*	15	18	23	20	26	21	20	18
England as whole to have its own new parliament with law-making powers	18	19	16	17	18	21	18	21
Unweighted base	*2718*	*1928*	*2761*	*2897*	*3709*	*2684*	*1794*	*928*

	2007	2008	2009	2010	2011	2012	2013	2015
Following is best for England...	%	%	%	%	%	%	%	%
England governed as it is now, with laws made by the UK parliament	57	51	49	53	56	56	56	51
Each region of England to have its own assembly that runs services like health*	14	15	15	13	12	15	15	22
England as whole to have its own new parliament with law-making powers	17	26	29	23	25	22	19	19
Unweighted base	*859*	*982*	*980*	*913*	*967*	*939*	*925*	*1865*

** In 2004–2006 the second option read "that makes decisions about the region's economy, planning and housing". The 2003 survey carried both versions of this option and demonstrated that the difference of wording did not make a material difference to the pattern of response. The figures quoted for 2003 are those for the two versions combined*

Base: Respondents in England only

The data on which Figure 6 is based are as follows:

Table A.6 Duty to vote, 1987-2015

	87	91	94	96	98	00	01	04
It is not really worth voting	3	8	9	8	8	11	11	12
People should only vote if they care who wins	21	24	21	26	26	24	23	27
It is every-one's duty to vote	76	68	68	64	65	64	65	60
Unweighted base	*3413*	*1224*	*970*	*989*	*1654*	*2008*	*2795*	*2609*

	05	08	09	10	11	13	15
It is not really worth voting	12	18	17	18	16	16	12
People should only vote if they care who wins	23	23	23	20	21	24	20
It is every-one's duty to vote	64	56	58	61	62	57	66
Unweighted base	*1732*	*990*	*1017*	*921*	*1909*	*904*	*1812*

Source: 1987: British Election Study

Bases for Table 6 are as follows:

Table A.7 Bases for political interest and electoral participation, 1997-2005

% who voted	1997	2001	2005	2010	2015
Interest in politics					
Unweighted base (Great deal/quite a lot)	*939*	*1009*	*1422*	*333*	*1551*
Unweighted base (Some)	*1066*	*1107*	*1484*	*369*	*1409*
Unweighted base (Not much/None at all)	*901*	*1171*	*1362*	*365*	*1365*

Bases for Table 7 are as follows:

Table A.8 Bases for turnout, by civic duty, 1987-2015

% who voted	1987	2001	2005	2010	2015
Unweighted base (It's not really worth voting)	*109*	*317*	*210*	*157*	*221*
Unweighted base (People should only vote if they care who wins)	*697*	*644*	*379*	*169*	*351*
Unweighted base (It's everyone's duty to vote)	*2586*	*1798*	*1122*	*579*	*1200*

Bases for Table 8 are as follows:

Table A.9 Bases for turnout by age, 1997-2015

	18-24	25-34	35-44	45-54	55-64	65+
% voted in						
Unweighted base (1997)	*316*	*580*	*566*	*518*	*386*	*532*
Unweighted base (2001)	*226*	*567*	*712*	*555*	*467*	*755*
Unweighted base (2005)	*330*	*627*	*870*	*713*	*730*	*996*
Unweighted base (2010)	*76*	*160*	*211*	*164*	*180*	*286*
Unweighted base (2015)	*290*	*635*	*728*	*764*	*711*	*1193*

The data on which Figure 7 is based are as follows:

Table A.10 Attitudes to taxation and spending on health, education and social benefits, 1983–2015

	1983	1984	1985	1986	1987	1988	1989	1990	1991	1992	1993
View on level of taxation and spending	%	%	%	%	%	%	%	%	%	%	%
Increase taxes/spend more	32	n/a	n/a	46	50	n/a	50	54	65	n/a	63
Keep taxes/ spend same	54	n/a	n/a	44	42	n/a	46	37	29	n/a	29
Reduce taxes/ spend less	9	n/a	n/a	5	3	n/a	3	3	3	n/a	4
Unweighted base	*1761*	*n/a*	*n/a*	*3100*	*2847*	*n/a*	*3029*	*2797*	*2918*	*n/a*	*2945*

	1994	1995	1996	1997	1998	1999	2000	2001	2002	2003	2004
View on level of taxation and spending	%	%	%	%	%	%	%	%	%	%	%
Increase taxes/spend more	58	61	59	62	63	58	50	59	63	51	49
Keep taxes/ spend same	33	31	34	31	32	35	40	34	31	38	42
Reduce taxes/ spend less	4	5	4	3	3	4	5	3	3	6	6
Unweighted base	*3469*	*3633*	*3620*	*1355*	*3146*	*3143*	*2292*	*3287*	*3435*	*3272*	*2146*

	2005	2006	2007	2008	2009	2010	2011	2012	2013	2014	2015
View on level of taxation and spending	%	%	%	%	%	%	%	%	%	%	%
Increase taxes/spend more	46	46	42	39	34	32	36	34	36	37	45
Keep taxes/ spend same	43	44	47	50	55	56	54	53	54	52	47
Reduce taxes/ spend less	7	6	7	8	8	8	6	6	6	7	4
Unweighted base	*2166*	*3240*	*3094*	*2229*	*1139*	*3297*	*3311*	*3248*	*3244*	*2878*	*3266*

n/a = not asked

Party political identification questions

The British Social Attitudes questions to ascertain party identification are as follows.

First, all respondents are asked:

> ***Generally speaking, do you think of yourself as a supporter of any one political party?***

Those who do not name a party in response are then asked:

> ***Do you think of yourself as a little closer to one political party than to the others?***

Those who still do not name a party are then asked:

> ***If there were a general election tomorrow, which political party do you think you would be most likely to support?***

Finally, all those who named a party at any of these questions are asked about the strength of their support or allegiance:

> ***Would you call yourself very strong (party), fairly strong, or not very strong?***

Technical details

In 2015, the sample for the British Social Attitudes survey was split into four equally-sized portions. Each portion was asked a different version of the questionnaire (versions A, B, C and D). Depending on the number of versions in which it was included, questions were thus asked either of the full sample (4,328 respondents) or of a random quarter, half or three-quarters of the sample.

Sample design

The British Social Attitudes survey is designed to yield a representative sample of adults aged 18 or over. Since 1993, the sampling frame for the survey has been the Postcode Address File (PAF), a list of addresses (or postal delivery points) compiled by the Post Office.[1]

For practical reasons, the sample is confined to those living in private households. People living in institutions (though not in private households at such institutions) are excluded, as are households whose addresses were not on the PAF.

The sampling method involved a multi-stage design, with three separate stages of selection.

Selection of sectors

At the first stage, postcode sectors were selected systematically from a list of all postal sectors in Britain. Before selection, any sectors with fewer than 500 addresses were identified and grouped together with an adjacent sector; in Scotland all sectors north of the Caledonian Canal were excluded (because of the prohibitive costs of interviewing there). Sectors were then stratified on the basis of: 37 sub-regions; population density, (population in private households/ area of the postal sector in hectares), with variable banding used in order to create three equal-sized strata per sub-region; and ranking by percentage of homes that were owner-occupied.

This resulted in the selection of 362 postcode sectors, with probability proportional to the number of addresses in each sector.

Selection of addresses

Twenty-six addresses were selected in each of the 362 sectors or groups of sectors. The issued sample was therefore 362 x 26 = 9,412 addresses, selected by starting from a random point on the list of addresses for each sector, and choosing each address at a fixed interval. The fixed interval was calculated for each sector in order to generate the correct number of addresses.

The Multiple-Occupancy Indicator (MOI) available through PAF was used when selecting addresses in Scotland. The MOI shows the number of accommodation spaces sharing one address. Thus, if the MOI indicated more than one accommodation space at a given address, the chances of the given address being selected from the list of addresses would increase so that it matched the total number of accommodation spaces. The MOI is largely irrelevant in England and Wales, as separate dwelling units (DUs) generally appear as separate entries on the PAF. In Scotland, tenements with many flats tend to appear as one entry on the PAF. However, even in Scotland, the vast majority (99.8%) of MOIs in the sample had a value of one. The remainder had MOIs greater than one. The MOI affects the selection probability of the address, so it was necessary to incorporate an adjustment for this into the weighting procedures (described below).

Selection of individuals

Interviewers called at each address selected from the PAF and listed all those eligible for inclusion in the British Social Attitudes sample – that is, all persons currently aged 18 or over and resident at the selected address. The interviewer then selected one respondent using a computer-generated random selection procedure. Where there were two or more DUs at the selected address, interviewers first had to select one DU using the same random procedure. They then followed the same procedure to select a person for interview within the selected DU.

Weighting

The weights for the British Social Attitudes survey correct for the unequal selection of addresses, DUs and individuals, and for biases caused by differential non-response. The different stages of the weighting scheme are outlined in detail below.

Selection weights

Selection weights are required because not all the units covered in the survey had the same probability of selection. The weighting reflects the relative selection probabilities of the individual at the three main stages of selection: address, DU and individual. First, because addresses in Scotland were selected using the MOI, weights were needed to compensate for the greater probability of an address with an MOI of more than one being selected, compared with an address with an MOI of one. (This stage was omitted for the English and Welsh data.) Secondly, data were weighted to compensate for the fact that a DU at an address that contained a large number of DUs was less likely to be selected for inclusion in the survey than a DU at an address that contained fewer DUs. (We used this procedure because in most cases where the MOI is greater than one, the two stages will cancel each other out, resulting in more efficient weights.) Thirdly, data were weighted to compensate for the lower selection probabilities of adults living in large households, compared with those in small households.

At each stage the selection weights were trimmed to avoid a small number of very high or very low weights in the sample; such weights would inflate standard errors, reducing the precision of the survey estimates and causing the weighted sample to be less efficient. Less than 1% of the selection weights were trimmed at each stage.

Non-response model

It is known that certain subgroups in the population are more likely to respond to surveys than others. These groups can end up over-represented in the sample, which can bias the survey estimates. Where information is available about non-responding households, the response behaviour of the sample members can be modelled and the results used to generate a non-response weight. This non-response weight is intended to reduce bias in the sample resulting from differential response to the survey.

The data was modelled using logistic regression, with the dependent variable indicating whether or not the selected individual responded to the survey. Ineligible households[2] were not included in the non-response modelling. A number of area-level and interviewer observation variables were used to model response. Not all the variables examined were retained for the final model: variables not strongly related to a household's propensity to respond were dropped from the analysis.

The variables found to be related to response were: region, the relative condition of the immediate local area, the relative condition of the address, whether there were entry barriers to the selected address, percentage of owner occupiers, and population density. The model shows that response increases if there are no barriers to entry (for instance, if there are no locked gates around the address and no entry phone) and if the general condition of the address is the same or better than other addresses in the area. Response decreases if the relative condition of the immediate surrounding area is mainly good or fair, and decreases as population density increases. Response is also higher for addresses in the North, the Midlands and the South East. The full model is given in Table A.1.

Table A.1 The final non-response model

Variable	B	S.E.	Wald	Df	Sig.	Odds
Region			80.171	11	.000	
Inner London	(baseline)					
North East	.553	.160	11.955	1	.001	1.738
North West	.627	.135	21.433	1	.000	1.871
Yorkshire and The Humber	.273	.143	3.640	1	.056	1.314
East Midlands	.786	.145	29.344	1	.000	2.195
West Midlands	.500	.141	12.495	1	.000	1.648
East of England	.394	.146	7.313	1	.007	1.482
Outer London	.309	.140	4.894	1	.027	1.362
South East	.600	.134	19.955	1	.000	1.822
South West	.443	.147	9.141	1	.002	1.558
Wales	.236	.159	2.211	1	.137	1.266
Scotland	.119	.142	0.706	1	.401	1.127
Barriers to address						
No barriers	(baseline)					
One or more	-.483	.088	30.085	1	.000	.617
Relative condition of the local area			18.430	2	.000	
Mainly good	(baseline)					
Mainly fair	-.160	.050	10.359	1	.001	.852
Mainly bad or very bad	-.462	.128	13.021	1	.000	.630
Relative condition of the address			38.411	2	0.000	
Better	(baseline)					
About the same	-.488	.085	32.695	1	.000	.614
Worse	-.660	.118	31.207	1	.000	.517
Percentage owner-occupied (in quintiles)			12.350	4	0.015	
1 lowest	(constant)					
2	-.137	.076	3.233	1	.072	.872
3	-.023	.080	.082	1	.774	.977
4	-.215	.086	6.323	1	.012	.807
5 highest	-.210	.087	5.778	1	.016	.811
Population density (population in private households/ area of postcode sector in hectares)	-.086	.024	13.141	1	.000	.917
Constant	.473	.179	6.968	1	.008	1.604

The response is 1 = individual responding to the survey, 0 = non-response

For consistency with previous years, region was also included in the non-response model. As region is used in the calibration weighting, including it in the non-response model can be beneficial in reducing the variance of the final weights

The model R^2 is 0.024 (Cox and Snell)

B** is the estimate coefficient with standard error **S.E.

*The **Wald**-test measures the impact of the categorical variable on the model with the appropriate number of degrees of freedom (**df**). If the test is significant (**sig.** < 0.05), then the categorical variable is considered to be 'significantly associated' with the response variable and therefore included in the model*

The non-response weight was calculated as the inverse of the predicted response probabilities saved from the logistic regression model. The non-response weight was then combined with the selection weights to create the final non-response weight. The top 1% of the weight were trimmed before the weight was scaled to the achieved sample size (resulting in the weight being standardised around an average of one).

Calibration weighting

The final stage of weighting was to adjust the final non-response weight so that the weighted sample matched the population in terms of age, sex and region.

Table A.2 Weighted and unweighted sample distribution, by region, age and sex

	Population	Unweighted respondents	Respondent weighted by selection weight only	Respondent weighted by un-calibrated non-response and selection weight	Respondent weighted by final weight
Region	%	%	%	%	%
North East	4.2	4.6	4.4	4.3	4.2
North West	11.3	12.8	12.7	11.7	11.3
Yorkshire and The Humber	8.5	7.9	7.4	8.1	8.5
East Midlands	7.4	10.1	10.0	8.6	7.4
West Midlands	9.0	9.0	9.1	9.0	9.0
East of England	9.6	8.2	8.6	8.6	9.6
London	13.4	9.9	10.3	12.2	13.4
South East	14.1	16.3	16.6	15.4	14.1
South West	8.8	8.7	8.4	8.2	8.8
Wales	5.0	5.0	4.8	5.2	5.0
Scotland	8.7	7.7	7.5	8.7	8.7
Age & sex	%	%	%	%	%
M 18–24	5.9	3.1	4.4	4.4	5.9
M 25–34	8.6	5.9	6.3	6.5	8.6
M 35–44	8.2	7.1	7.3	7.2	8.2
M 45–54	8.8	8.0	8.4	8.4	8.8
M 55–59	3.7	3.0	3.3	3.3	3.7
M 60–64	3.4	4.0	4.1	4.0	3.4
M 65+	10.1	12.8	11.7	11.5	10.1
F 18–24	5.7	3.6	4.3	4.4	5.7
F 25–34	8.6	8.8	8.5	8.8	8.6
F 35–44	8.3	9.7	10.0	10.0	8.3
F 45–54	9.1	9.6	10.2	10.2	9.1
F 55–59	3.8	4.9	4.9	4.9	3.8
F 60–64	3.5	4.5	4.4	4.2	3.5
F 65+	12.3	14.9	12.2	12.1	12.3
Base	*49,501,761*	*4328*	*4328*	*4328*	*4328*

Only adults aged 18 or over are eligible to take part in the survey, therefore the data have been weighted to the British population aged 18+ based on 2011 Census data from the Office for National Statistics/General Register Office for Scotland.

The survey data were weighted to the marginal age/sex and GOR distributions using raking-ratio (or rim) weighting. As a result, the weighted data should exactly match the population across these three dimensions. This is shown in Table A.2.

The calibration weight is the final non-response weight to be used in the analysis of the 2015 survey; this weight has been scaled to the responding sample size. The range of the weights is given in Table A.3.

Table A.3 Range of weights

	N	Minimum	Mean	Maximum
DU and person selection weight	4328	.56	1.00	2.23
Un-calibrated non-response and selection weight	4328	.38	1.00	3.47
Final calibrated non-response weight	4328	.27	1.00	4.91

Effective sample size

The effect of the sample design on the precision of survey estimates is indicated by the effective sample size (neff). The effective sample size measures the size of an (unweighted) simple random sample that would achieve the same precision (standard error) as the design being implemented. If the effective sample size is close to the actual sample size, then we have an efficient design with a good level of precision. The lower the effective sample size is, the lower the level of precision. The efficiency of a sample is given by the ratio of the effective sample size to the actual sample size. Samples that select one person per household tend to have lower efficiency than samples that select all household members. The final calibrated non-response weights have an effective sample size (neff) of 3,486 and efficiency of 81%.

Weighted bases

All the percentages presented in this report are based on weighted data. Only unweighted bases are presented in the tables. Details of weighted bases for standard demographics are shown in Table A.4.

Table A.4 Weighted and unweighted bases for standard demographics, 2015

	Weighted base	*Unweighted base*
Sex		
Male	2105	1904
Female	2223	2424
Age		
18-24	500	290
25-34	743	635
35-44	712	728
45-54	776	764
55-59	326	344
60-64	299	367
65+	966	1193
Ethnicity		
White	3746	3861
Non-White	529	424
Religion		
No religion	2097	2067
Church of England/Anglican	736	850
Other Christian	740	758
Non-Christian	364	275
Roman Catholic	375	364
Class group (NSSEC)		
Managerial & professional occupations	1617	1619
Intermediate occupations	495	532
Employers in small org; own account workers	383	380
Lower supervisory & technical occupations	404	392
Semi-routine & routine occupations	1213	1241
Highest educational qualification		
Degree	1033	980
Higher education below degree	474	487
A level or equivalent	832	743
O level or equivalent	804	794
CSE or equivalent	307	318
Foreign or other	101	94
No qualification	766	903
Marital status		
Married	2120	1905
Living as married	500	401
Separated or divorced after marrying	402	623
Widowed	276	440
Not married	1027	957

Questionnaire versions

Each address in each sector (sampling point) was allocated to one of the portions of the sample: A, B, C or D. As mentioned earlier, a different version of the questionnaire was used with each of the four sample portions. If one serial number was version A, the next was version B, the next version C, and the fourth version D. There were 2,353 issued addresses for each of the four versions of the sample.

Fieldwork

Interviewing was mainly carried out between August and October 2015, with a small number of interviews taking place in November 2015.

Fieldwork was conducted by interviewers drawn from NatCen Social Research's regular panel and conducted using face-to-face computer-assisted interviewing.[3] Interviewers attended a one-day briefing conference to familiarise them with the selection procedures and questionnaires, with the exception of experienced interviewers who completed a self-briefing containing updates to the questionnaire and procedures.

The mean interview length was 67 minutes for version A of the questionnaire, 62 minutes for version B, 65 minutes for version C, and 64 minutes for version D.[4] Interviewers achieved an overall response rate of between 51.0 and 51.4%. Details are shown in Table A.5.

Table A.5 Response rate[1] on British Social Attitudes, 2015

	Number	Lower limit of response (%)	Upper limit of response (%)
Addresses issued	9412		
Out of scope	923		
Upper limit of eligible cases	8489	100	
Uncertain eligibility	61	0.7	
Lower limit of eligible cases	8428		100
Interview achieved	4328	51.0	51.4
With self-completion	3670	43.2	43.5
Interview not achieved	4100	48.3	48.6
Refused[2]	3148	37.1	37.4
Non-contacted[3]	448	5.3	5.3
Other non-response	503	5.9	6.0

1 Response is calculated as a range from a lower limit where all unknown eligibility cases (for example, address inaccessible, or unknown whether address is residential) are assumed to be eligible and therefore included in the unproductive outcomes, to an upper limit where all these cases are assumed to be ineligible and therefore excluded from the response calculation

2 'Refused' comprises refusals before selection of an individual at the address, refusals to the office, refusal by the selected person, 'proxy' refusals (on behalf of the selected respondent) and broken appointments after which the selected person could not be recontacted

3 'Non-contacted' comprises households where no one was contacted and those where the selected person could not be contacted

As in earlier rounds of the series, the respondent was asked to fill in a self-completion questionnaire which, whenever possible, was collected by the interviewer. Otherwise, the respondent was asked to post it to NatCen Social Research.

A total of 658 respondents (15% of those interviewed) did not return their self-completion questionnaire. Version A of the self-completion questionnaire was returned by 86% of respondents to the face-to-face interview, version B of the questionnaire was returned by 84%, version C by 86%, and version D by 84%. As in previous rounds, we judged that it was not necessary to apply additional weights to correct for non-response to the self-completion questionnaire.

Advance letter

Advance letters describing the purpose of the survey and the coverage of the questionnaire, were sent to sampled addresses before the interviewer made their first call.[5]

Analysis variables

A number of standard analyses have been used in the tables that appear in this report. The analysis groups requiring further definition are set out below. For further details see Stafford and Thomson (2006). Where relevant the name given to the relevant analysis variable is shown in square brackets – for example [REarn].

Region

The dataset is classified by 12 regions, formerly the Government Office Regions.

Standard Occupational Classification

Respondents are classified according to their own occupation, not that of the 'head of household'. Each respondent was asked about their current or last job, so that all respondents except those who had never worked were coded. Additionally, all job details were collected for all spouses and partners in work.

Since the 2011 survey, we have coded occupation to the Standard Occupational Classification 2010 (SOC 2010) instead of the Standard Occupational Classification 2000 (SOC 2000). The main socio-economic grouping based on SOC 2010 is the National Statistics Socio-Economic Classification (NS-SEC). However, to maintain time-series, some analysis has continued to use the older schemes based on SOC 90 – Registrar General's Social Class and Socio-Economic Group – though these are now derived from SOC 2000 (which is derived from SOC 2010).

National Statistics Socio-Economic Classification (NS-SEC)

The combination of SOC 2010 and employment status for current or last job generates the following NS-SEC analytic classes:

- Employers in large organisations, higher managerial and professional
- Lower professional and managerial; higher technical and supervisory
- Intermediate occupations
- Small employers and own account workers
- Lower supervisory and technical occupations
- Semi-routine occupations
- Routine occupations

The remaining respondents are grouped as "never had a job" or "not classifiable". For some analyses, it may be more appropriate to classify respondents according to their current socio-economic status, which takes into account only their present economic position. In this case, in addition to the seven classes listed above, the remaining respondents not currently in paid work fall into one of the following categories: "not classifiable", "retired", "looking after the home", "unemployed" or "others not in paid occupations".

Registrar General's Social Class

As with NS-SEC, each respondent's social class is based on his or her current or last occupation. The combination of SOC 90 with employment status for current or last job generates the following six social classes:

I		Professional etc. occupations	'Non-manual'
II		Managerial and technical occupations	
III	(Non-manual)	Skilled occupations	
III	(Manual)	Skilled occupations	'Manual'
IV		Partly skilled occupations	
V		Unskilled occupations	

They are usually collapsed into four groups: I & II, III Non-manual, III Manual, and IV & V.

Socio-Economic Group

As with NS-SEC, each respondent's Socio-Economic Group (SEG) is based on his or her current or last occupation. SEG aims to bring together people with jobs of similar social and economic status, and is derived from a combination of employment status and occupation. The full SEG classification identifies 18 categories, but these are usually condensed into six groups:

- Professionals, employers and managers
- Intermediate non-manual workers
- Junior non-manual workers
- Skilled manual workers
- Semi-skilled manual workers
- Unskilled manual workers

As with NS-SEC, the remaining respondents are grouped as "never had a job" or "not classifiable".

Industry

All respondents whose occupation could be coded were allocated a Standard Industrial Classification 2007 (SIC 07). Two-digit class codes are used. As with social class, SIC may be generated on the basis of the respondent's current occupation only, or on his or her most recently classifiable occupation.

Party identification

Respondents can be classified as identifying with a particular political party on one of three counts: if they consider themselves supporters of that party, closer to it than to others, or more likely to support it in the event of a general election. The three groups are generally described respectively as 'partisans', 'sympathisers' and 'residual identifiers'. In combination, the three groups are referred to as 'identifiers'. Responses are derived from the following questions:

> ***Generally speaking, do you think of yourself as a supporter of any one political party? [Yes/No]***
>
> ***[If "No"/"Don't know"]***
>
> ***Do you think of yourself as a little closer to one political party than to the others? [Yes/No]***
>
> ***[If "Yes" at either question or "No"/"Don't know" at 2nd question]***
>
> ***Which one?/If there were a general election tomorrow, which political party do you think you would be most likely to support?***
>
> ***[Conservative; Labour; Liberal Democrat; Scottish National Party; Plaid Cymru; Green Party; UK Independence Party (UKIP)/Veritas; British National Party (BNP)/National Front; RESPECT/Scottish Socialist Party (SSP)/Socialist Party; Other party; Other answer; None; Refused to say]***

Income

Two variables classify the respondent's earnings [REarn] and household income [HHInc] The bandings used are designed to be representative of those that exist in Britain and are taken from the Family Resources Survey (see http://research.dwp.gov.uk/asd/frs/). Four derived variables give income deciles/quartiles: [RearnD], [REarnQ], [HHIncD] and [HHIncQ]. Deciles and quartiles are calculated based on individual earnings and household incomes in Britain as a whole.

Attitude scales

Since 1986, the British Social Attitudes surveys have included two attitude scales which aim to measure where respondents stand on certain underlying value dimensions – left–right and libertarian–authoritarian.[6] Since 1987 (except in 1990), a similar scale on 'welfarism' has also been included. Some of the items in the welfarism scale were changed in 2000–2001. The current version of the scale is shown below.

A useful way of summarising the information from a number of questions of this sort is to construct an additive index (Spector, 1992; DeVellis, 2003). This approach rests on the assumption that there is an underlying – 'latent' – attitudinal dimension which characterises the answers to all the questions within each scale. If so, scores on the index are likely to be a more reliable indication of the underlying attitude than the answers to any one question.

Each of these scales consists of a number of statements to which the respondent is invited to "agree strongly", "agree", "neither agree nor disagree", "disagree" or "disagree strongly".

The items are:

Left–right scale

Government should redistribute income from the better off to those who are less well off [Redistrb]

Big business benefits owners at the expense of workers [BigBusnN]

Ordinary working people do not get their fair share of the nation's wealth [Wealth][7]

There is one law for the rich and one for the poor [RichLaw]

Management will always try to get the better of employees if it gets the chance [Indust4]

Libertarian–authoritarian scale

Young people today don't have enough respect for traditional British values. [TradVals]

People who break the law should be given stiffer sentences. [StifSent]

For some crimes, the death penalty is the most appropriate sentence. [DeathApp]

Schools should teach children to obey authority. [Obey]

The law should always be obeyed, even if a particular law is wrong. [WrongLaw]

Censorship of films and magazines is necessary to uphold moral standards. [Censor]

Welfarism scale

The welfare state encourages people to stop helping each other. [WelfHelp]

The government should spend more money on welfare benefits for the poor, even if it leads to higher taxes. [MoreWelf]

Around here, most unemployed people could find a job if they really wanted one. [UnempJob]

Many people who get social security don't really deserve any help. [SocHelp]

Most people on the dole are fiddling in one way or another. [DoleFidl]

If welfare benefits weren't so generous, people would learn to stand on their own two feet. [WelfFeet]

Cutting welfare benefits would damage too many people's lives. [DamLives]

The creation of the welfare state is one of Britain's proudest achievements. [ProudWlf]

The indices for the three scales are formed by scoring the leftmost, most libertarian or most pro-welfare position, as 1 and the rightmost, most authoritarian or most anti-welfarist position, as 5. The "neither agree nor disagree" option is scored as 3. The scores to all the questions in each scale are added and then divided by the number of items in the scale, giving indices ranging from 1 (leftmost, most libertarian, most pro-welfare) to 5 (rightmost, most authoritarian, most anti-welfare). The scores on the three indices have been placed on the dataset.[8]

The scales have been tested for reliability (as measured by Cronbach's alpha). The Cronbach's alpha (unstandardised items) for the scales in 2014 are 0.82 for the left–right scale, 0.82 for the welfarism scale and 0.74 for the libertarian–authoritarian scale. This level of reliability can be considered "good" for the left–right and libertarian–authoritarian scales and "respectable" for the welfarism scale (DeVellis, 2003: 95–96).

Other analysis variables

These are taken directly from the questionnaire and to that extent are self-explanatory The principal ones are:

- Sex
- Age
- Household income
- Economic position
- Religion
- Highest educational qualification obtained
- Marital status
- Benefits received

Sampling errors

No sample precisely reflects the characteristics of the population it represents, because of both sampling and non-sampling errors. If a sample were designed as a random sample (if every adult had an equal and independent chance of inclusion in the sample), then we could calculate the sampling error of any percentage, ***p***, using the formula:

$$\text{s.e. (p)} = \sqrt{\frac{p(100 - p)}{n}}$$

where *n* is the number of respondents on which the percentage is based. Once the sampling error had been calculated, it would be a straightforward exercise to calculate a confidence interval for the true population percentage. For example, a 95% confidence interval would be given by the formula:

$p \pm 1.96 \times \text{s.e. (p)}$

Clearly, for a simple random sample (srs), the sampling error depends only on the values of ***p*** and ***n***. However, simple random sampling is almost never used in practice, because of its inefficiency in terms of time and cost.

As noted above, the British Social Attitudes sample, like that drawn for most large-scale surveys, was clustered according to a stratified multi-stage design into 261postcode sectors (or combinations of sectors). With a complex design like this, the sampling error of a percentage giving a particular response is not simply a function of the number of respondents in the sample and the size of the percentage; it also depends on how that percentage response is spread within and between sample points.

$$\text{DEFT} = \sqrt{\frac{\text{Variance of estimator with complex design, sample size n}}{\text{Variance of estimator with srs design, sample size n}}}$$

The complex design may be assessed relative to simple random sampling by calculating a range of design factors (DEFTs) associated with it, where:

and represents the multiplying factor to be applied to the simple random sampling error to produce its complex equivalent. A design factor of one means that the complex sample has achieved the same precision as a simple random sample of the same size. A design factor greater than one means the complex sample is less precise than its simple random sample equivalent. If the DEFT for a particular characteristic is known, a 95% confidence interval for a percentage may be calculated using the formula:

p ± 1.96 x complex sampling error (p)

$$= p \pm 1.96 \times \text{DEFT} \times \sqrt{\frac{p(100 - p)}{n}}$$

Table A.6 gives examples of the confidence intervals and DEFTs calculated for a range of different questions. Most background questions were asked of the whole sample, whereas many attitudinal questions were asked only of a third or two-thirds of the sample; some were asked on the interview questionnaire and some on the self-completion supplement.

Table A.6 Complex standard errors and confidence intervals of selected variables

	% (p)	Complex standard error of p	95% confidence interval	DEFT	*Base*
Classification variables					
Party identification (full sample)					
Conservative	31.5	.9	29.8-33.4	1.288	*4326*
Labour	29.8	.9	28.0-31.7	1.322	*4326*
UKIP	5.5	.4	4.7-6.3	1.163	*4326*
Liberal Democrat	4.5	.4	3.8-5.4	1.323	*4326*
Scottish National Party	3.3	.3	2.8-4.0	1.082	*4326*
UK Independence Party	5.5	.4	4.7-6.3	1.163	*4326*
None	14.6	.8	13.1-16.2	1.467	*4326*
Housing tenure (full sample)					
Owns	63.9	1.1	61.7-66.1	1.520	*4328*
Rents from local authority	9.9	.7	8.6-11.3	1.463	*4328*
Rents privately/HA	24.9	1.0	23.0-26.8	1. 466	*4328*
Religion (full sample)					
No religion	48.5	1.0	46.5-50.5	1.343	*4328*
Church of England	17.0	.7	15.7-18.4	1.231	*4328*
Roman Catholic	8.7	.5	7.7-9.7	1.154	*4328*
Age of completing continuous full-time education (full sample)					
16 or under	44.9	1.1	42.7-47.0	1.422	*4328*
17 or 18	21.5	.8	20.0-23.1	1.283	*4328*
19 or over	28.9	1.0	27.1-30.9	1.392	*4328*

	% (p)	Complex standard error of p	95% confidence interval	DEFT	*Base*
Can I just check, would you describe the place where you live as... (full sample)					
...a big city	11.5	1.0	9.6-13.7	2.120	*4328*
the suburbs or outskirts of a big city	23.8	1.5	21.1-26.8	2.254	*4328*
a small city or town	44.7	1.7	41.3-48.1	2.282	*4328*
a country village	17.2	1.3	14.8-19.9	2.262	*4328*
or, a farm or home in the country?	2.1	.3	1.6-2.7	1.279	*4328*
Attitudinal variables (face-to-face interview)					
Benefits for the unemployed are … (three-quarters of sample)					
… too low	23.5	.8	21.9-25.2	1.133	*3266*
… too high	58.8	1.0	56.7-60.8	1.195	*3266*
How serious a problem is traffic congestion in towns, cities (three-quarters of sample)					
A very serious problem	16.8	.7	15.4-18.3	1.133	*3223*
A serious problem	37.7	1.0	35.7-39.8	1.205	*3223*
Not a very serious problem	32.5	1.0	30.6-34.5	1.204	*3223*
Not a problem at all	12.8	.7	11.5-14.3	1.231	*3223*
How much interest do you generally have in what is going on in politics… (full sample)					
... a great deal	11.7	.6	10.6-12.8	1.159	*4328*
quite a lot	24.1	.8	22.6-25.7	1.219	*4328*
some	32.6	.9	30.9-34.3	1.198	*4328*
not very much	19.9	.7	18.5-21.4	1.225	*4328*
or, none at all?	11.6	.7	10.3-13.1	1.473	*4328*
Please say how much you agree or disagree with the following statements. 'There is no reason to worry about being a bit overweight'? (one half of sample)					
Agree strongly	4.4	.5	3.4-5.6	1.240	*2188*
Agree	41.9	1.3	39.3-44.6	1.266	*2188*
Neither agree nor disagree	10.6	.7	9.3-12.0	1.069	*2188*
Disagree	34.4	1.2	32.1-36.9	1.204	*2188*
Disagree strongly	8.6	.7	7.3-10.1	1.183	*2188*
Attitudinal variables (self-completion)					
Government should redistribute income from the better off to those who are less well off (full sample)					
Agree strongly	11.8	.6	10.6-13.2	1.201	*3670*
Agree	32.0	.8	30.3-33.7	1.089	*3670*
Neither agree nor disagree	28.2	.9	26.5-30.0	1.203	*3670*
Disagree	21.2	.8	19.7-22.9	1.213	*3670*
Disagree strongly	4.7	.4	4.0-5.5	1.124	*3670*
Some working couples with children find it hard to make ends meet on low wages. In these circumstances, do you think … (three-quarters of sample)					
…the government should top-up their wages	55.3	1.1	53.2-57.4	1.132	*2781*
…or, is it up to the couple to look after themselves and their children as best they can?	29.4	1.0	27.4-31.4	1.178	*2781*
Can't choose	14.1	.7	12.8-15.6	1.089	*2781*

	% (p)	Complex standard error of p	95% confidence interval	DEFT	*Base*
People should be able to travel by plane as much as they like (one quarter of sample)					
Agree	62.7	1.7	59.3-66.1	1.075	*889*
Neither agree nor disagree	23.3	1.4	20.5-26.2	1.011	*889*
Disagree	6.7	1.1	4.9-9.1	1.264	*889*

The table shows that most of the questions asked of all sample members have a confidence interval of around plus or minus two to four of the survey percentage. This means that we can be 95% certain that the true population percentage is within two to four per cent (in either direction) of the percentage we report.

Variables with much larger variation are, as might be expected, those closely related to the geographic location of the respondent (for example, whether they live in a big city, a small town or a village). Here, the variation may be as large as six or seven per cent either way around the percentage found on the survey. Consequently, the design effects calculated for these variables in a clustered sample will be greater than the design effects calculated for variables less strongly associated with area. Also, sampling errors for percentages based only on respondents to just one of the versions of the questionnaire, or on subgroups within the sample, are larger than they would have been had the questions been asked of everyone.

Analysis techniques

Regression

Regression analysis aims to summarise the relationship between a 'dependent' variable and one or more 'independent' variables. It shows how well we can estimate a respondent's score on the dependent variable from knowledge of their scores on the independent variables. It is often undertaken to support a claim that the phenomena measured by the independent variables ***cause*** the phenomenon measured by the dependent variable. However, the causal ordering, if any, between the variables cannot be verified or falsified by the technique. Causality can only be inferred through special experimental designs or through assumptions made by the analyst.

All regression analysis assumes that the relationship between the dependent and each of the independent variables takes a particular form. In *linear regression*, it is assumed that the relationship can be adequately summarised by a straight line. This means that a one percentage point increase in the value of an independent variable is assumed to have the same impact on the value of the dependent variable on average, irrespective of the previous values of those variables.

Strictly speaking the technique assumes that both the dependent and the independent variables are measured on an interval-level scale, although it may sometimes still be applied even where this is not the case. For example, one can use an ordinal variable (e.g. a Likert scale) as a *dependent* variable if one is willing to assume that there is an underlying interval-level scale and the difference between the observed ordinal scale and the underlying interval scale is due to random measurement error. Often the answers to a number of Likert-type questions are averaged to give a dependent variable that is more like a continuous variable. Categorical or nominal data can be used as *independent* variables by converting them into dummy or binary variables; these are variables where the only valid scores are 0 and 1, with 1 signifying membership of a particular category and 0 otherwise.

The assumptions of linear regression cause particular difficulties where the *dependent* variable is binary. The assumption that the relationship between the dependent and the independent variables is a straight line means that it can produce estimated values for the dependent variable of less than 0 or greater than 1. In this case it may be more appropriate to assume that the relationship between the dependent and the independent variables takes the form of an S-curve, where the impact on the dependent variable of a one-point increase in an independent variable becomes progressively less the closer the value of the dependent variable approaches 0 or 1. *Logistic regression* is an alternative form of regression which fits such an S-curve rather than a straight line. The technique can also be adapted to analyse multinomial non-interval-level dependent variables, that is, variables which classify respondents into more than two categories.

The two statistical scores most commonly reported from the results of regression analyses are:

A measure of variance explained: This summarises how well all the independent variables combined can account for the variation in respondents' scores in the dependent variable. The higher the measure, the more accurately we are able in general to estimate the correct value of each respondent's score on the dependent variable from knowledge of their scores on the independent variables.

A parameter estimate: This shows how much the dependent variable will change on average, given a one-unit change in the independent variable (while holding all other independent variables in the model constant). The parameter estimate has a positive sign if an increase in the value of the independent variable results in an increase in the value of the dependent variable. It has a negative sign if an increase in the value of the independent variable results in a decrease in the value of the dependent variable. If the parameter estimates are standardised, it is possible to compare the relative impact of different independent variables; those variables with the largest standardised estimates can be said to have the biggest impact on the value of the dependent variable.

Regression also tests for the statistical significance of parameter estimates. A parameter estimate is said to be significant at the 5% level if the range of the values encompassed by its 95% confidence interval (see also section on sampling errors) are either all positive or all negative. This means that there is less than a 5% chance that the association we have found between the dependent variable and the independent variable is simply the result of sampling error and does not reflect a relationship that actually exists in the general population.

Factor analysis

Factor analysis is a statistical technique which aims to identify whether there are one or more apparent sources of commonality to the answers given by respondents to a set of questions. It ascertains the smallest number of ***factors*** (or dimensions) which can most economically summarise all of the variation found in the set of questions being analysed. Factors are established where respondents who gave a particular answer to one question in the set tended to give the same answer as each other to one or more of the other questions in the set. The technique is most useful when a relatively small number of factors are able to account for a relatively large proportion of the variance in all of the questions in the set.

The technique produces a ***factor loading*** for each question (or variable) on each factor. Where questions have a high loading on the same factor, then it will be the case that respondents who gave a particular answer to one of these questions tended to give a similar answer to each other at the other questions. The technique is most commonly used in attitudinal research to try to identify the underlying ideological dimensions which apparently structure attitudes towards the subject in question.

International Social Survey Programme

The International Social Survey Programme (ISSP) is run by a group of research organisations in different countries, each of which undertakes to field annually an agreed module of questions on a chosen topic area. Since 1985, an International Social Survey Programme module has been included in one of the British Social Attitudes self-completion questionnaires. Each module is chosen for repetition at intervals to allow comparisons both between countries (membership is currently standing at 48) and over time. In 2015, the chosen subject was Work orientations, and the module was carried on the B and D versions of the self-completion questionnaire (JbErnMny – AgeYngC).

Notes

1. Until 1991 all British Social Attitudes samples were drawn from the Electoral Register (ER). However, following concern that this sampling frame might be deficient in its coverage of certain population subgroups, a 'splicing' experiment was conducted in 1991. We are grateful to the Market Research Development Fund for contributing towards the costs of this experiment. Its purpose was to investigate whether a switch to PAF would disrupt the time-series – for instance, by lowering response rates or affecting the distribution of responses to particular questions. In the event, it was concluded that the change from ER to PAF was unlikely to affect time trends in any noticeable ways, and that no adjustment factors were necessary. Since significant differences in efficiency exist between PAF and ER, and because we considered it untenable to continue to use a frame that is known to be biased, we decided to adopt PAF as the sampling frame for future British Social Attitudes surveys. For details of the PAF/ER 'splicing' experiment, see Lynn and Taylor (1995).
2. This includes households not containing any adults aged 18 or over, vacant dwelling units, derelict dwelling units, non-resident addresses and other deadwood.
3. In 1993 it was decided to mount a split-sample experiment designed to test the applicability of Computer-Assisted Personal Interviewing (CAPI) to the British Social Attitudes survey series. CAPI has been used increasingly over the past decade as an alternative to traditional interviewing techniques. As the name implies, CAPI involves the use of a laptop computer during the interview, with the interviewer entering responses directly into the computer. One of the advantages of CAPI is that it significantly reduces both the amount of time spent on data processing and the number of coding and editing errors. There was, however, concern that a different interviewing technique might alter the distribution of responses and so affect the year-on-year consistency of British Social Attitudes data.

   Following the experiment, it was decided to change over to CAPI completely in 1994 (the self-completion questionnaire still being administered in the conventional way). The results of the experiment are discussed in the British Social Attitudes 11th Report (Lynn and Purdon, 1994).
4. Interview times recorded as less than 20 minutes were excluded, as these timings were likely to be errors.
5. An experiment was conducted on the 1991 British Social Attitudes survey (Jowell ***et al.***, 1992) which showed that sending advance letters to sampled addresses before fieldwork begins has very little impact on response rates. However, interviewers do find that an advance letter helps them to introduce the survey on the doorstep, and a majority of respondents have said that they preferred some advance notice. For these reasons, advance letters have been used on the British Social Attitudes surveys since 1991.

6. Because of methodological experiments on scale development, the exact items detailed in this section have not been asked on all versions of the questionnaire each year.
7. In 1994 only, this item was replaced by: Ordinary people get their fair share of the nation's wealth *[Wealth1].*
8. In constructing the scale, a decision had to be taken on how to treat missing values ("Don't know" and "Not answered"). Respondents who had more than two missing values on the left–right scale and more than three missing values on the libertarian–authoritarian and welfarism scales were excluded from that scale. For respondents with fewer missing values, "Don't know" was recoded to the midpoint of the scale and "Not answered" was recoded to the scale mean for that respondent on their valid items.

References

DeVellis, R.F. (2003), *Scale Development: Theory and Applications*, 2nd edition, Applied Social Research Methods Series, 26, Thousand Oaks, California: Sage

Jowell, R., Brook, L., Prior, G. and Taylor, B. (1992), *British Social Attitudes: the 9th Report*, Aldershot: Dartmouth

Lynn, P. and Purdon, S. (1994), 'Time-series and lap-tops: the change to computer- assisted interviewing', in Jowell, R., Curtice, J., Brook, L. and Ahrendt, D. (eds.), *British Social Attitudes: the 11th Report*, Aldershot: Dartmouth

Lynn, P. and Taylor, B. (1995), 'On the bias and variance of samples of individuals: a comparison of the Electoral Registers and Postcode Address File as sampling frames', *The Statistician*, 44: 173–194

Spector, P. (1992), *Summated Rating Scale Construction: An Introduction, Quantitative Applications in the Social Sciences*, 82, Newbury Park, California: Sage

Stafford, R. and Thomson, K. (2006), *British Social Attitudes and Young People's Social Attitudes surveys 2003: Technical Report*, London: NatCen Social Research